The Complete Parish

A Recipe for Success

Thomas F. Gull

J. S. Paluch Company, Inc.

In those days a decree went out from Caesar Augustus

    That the whole world should be enrolled.

This was the first enrollment,

    when Quirinius was governor of Syria.

So all went to be enrolled, each to his own town.

— Luke 2:1–3

Table of Contents

Chapter Two
Financial Information:
The Key to Funding Your Parish

Chapter Three
Parish Survey:
The Key to Understanding Your Parish

Chapter Four
Communication:
The Key to Explaining Your Parish

Chapter Five
Public Information:
The Key to Publicizing Your Parish

Chapter Six
Sacraments and Funerals:
The Key to Changing Your Parish

Chapter Seven
Spiritual Activities:
The Key to Enriching Your Parish

Chapter Eight
Service Activities:
The Key to Humanizing Your Parish

Chapter Nine
Social Activities:
The Key to Enlivening Your Parish

Appendix A:
Sample Confidential
Parish Census Form

Appendix B:
Resources

Introduction

Is there anyone who has not utilized the recommendations found in the pages of a self-help or "how to" book? Whether it is a cookbook or home improvement manual, a step-by-step guide to a better golf swing, a diet book, a business development text, or a new approach to personal growth, most everyone has turned to such a book at one time or another.

Can such a book have a positive impact on the development and growth of a parish? At first glance it might seem impractical or even inappropriate to turn to a self-help or "how to" book for spiritual matters. In fact, religious self-help books abound. How to pray better, understand the Mass, or be more charitable are just a few topics of interest to many Catholic faithful. Books about encouraging congregations to sing, teaching religion more creatively, or finding productive volunteers provide new ideas to parish staff members. Pastors have shelves filled with books about preaching more effectively. There are countless books for chaplains and volunteer ministers advising them of ways to serve people better.

This book offers ideas for parish staff members and especially parish business managers. It explains how they can use the wealth of data the parish routinely collects, along with readily available demographic data and local information, to reach more people and spread the message of the parish's programs and services more widely.

Better collection and utilization of standard—and readily available—demographic information is one key to developing a parish into a more effective, enriching faith community. As a parish staff begins to analyze this data, they will begin to understand their congregation better.

Data collection and utilization alone are not the answer to parish growth. The best software system and the fullest databank are of little value if people are not made to feel welcome or if the weekend liturgies are celebrated without preparation and a prayerful spirit. At the same time, the finest choir and the best preaching will not fill the church benches unless there is an organized effort by the business manager and parish staff to spread the message about the parish and its services to both existing and potential parishioners.

The first principle of this book is that a parish needs a current and complete database filled with information about its parishioners. The first and largest chapter explains how to collect the data and what information needs to be gathered.

The second principle is that utilizing the data correctly is essential for the success of every outreach effort and every parish program. Whether it is a financial, sacramental, spiritual, service, or social program, event, or activity, the data contained in the parish records and census is the key, both to judging the need for each program and as the means of attracting the potential audience.

Think of this book as a bible for business managers. It then becomes their mission to spread the message about the importance of gathering and utilizing parish data and to share the available information with the other members of the parish staff.

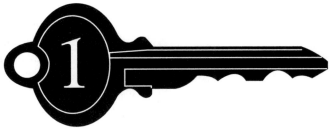

Parish Census Data:
The Key to Developing Your Parish

After being an active parishioner for eleven years, I was given the unique opportunity to join our parish staff in the newly created position of business manager. As someone who had worked in customer service and sales, as well as being a person with an innate knack for numbers and organization, I knew it would be a good fit for both the parish community and me. I had a personal sense of faith, an understanding of the general mission of the church, and a working knowledge of the particular challenges faced by my parish as it served the needs of a diverse faith community.

When I started my job as parish business manager, one of the things that really surprised me was the enormous amount of data kept at the parish. The original sacramental record books going back to the founding of the parish in 1907 were a fascinating treasure trove of information. There was also a card catalogue cross-referenced by street and last name, and a computer system filled with all the information from the parish census. The other surprise, however, was how little this data was being used. Parish staff and volunteer leaders knew many parishioners by name or by face. The parish staff offered countless spiritual and social services and activities, but rarely turned to the wealth of readily available parish data to determine whether they were reaching all or even a significant majority of the parish—or one of its many diverse segments.

Better collection and utilization of standard—and readily available—demographic information is a key to developing a parish into a more effective, enriching faith community. For their part, the parish staff and especially the parish business manager are the ones who need to gather, organize, and interpret this data. As a parish staff begins to analyze data, they will begin to understand their congregation better.

Too often parishes try to be all things to all people. Accomplishing this would require an unending supply of volunteers and a limitless budget. By carefully analyzing available data, a parish leadership team will uncover groups of people that they had not differentiated, served, or reached out to in an effective manner. A study of the demographic data may also answer some questions or concerns about why more people are not participating in a specific event. There may not be as many old, young, married, or single people in the parish as staff members might imagine.

By evaluating the demographic make-up of your parish, you might answer similar questions or discover the need for additional ministries, programs, or outreaches.

1.1. Gathering Parish Census Data

Many people are very organized and immediately upon moving into a new neighborhood march down the street and register with their local church. Others might shop around a while and when they finally settle in after ten years or so, complete a parish registration form. It can be a challenge to get people to commit their time, talent, and resources to a parish as a registered member. There are several different approaches that can foster registration.

Place registration packets and pencils in the pews on a given Sunday. Make a special announcement encouraging people to register. Point out the positive benefits: lower fees for weddings and funerals, inclusion in parish mailings—including collection envelopes and advance notice of opportunities to volunteer one's time!

Consider using Pentecost Sunday, with its focus on the founding of the church, or the solemnity of the Baptism of the Lord, with its sense of new beginning, as days to emphasize parish involvement, commitment, and registration.

Bribes work. Offer a box of chocolates to everyone who registers after Mass. One parish tried that and nearly thirty families and singles were gained that day!

A bulletin announcement and an abbreviated registration form printed in the bulletin might catch the eye of some people. Some parishes will do this once a month and consider it a good use of valuable space. Inserting a complete registration form into the bulletin occasionally might get others to sign up. Here's a sample announcement that can be modified and either printed in the bulletin or read from the pulpit.

Register Today:
Your Parish Needs You

Are you a registered parishioner? Last week two future grooms and an adult who was asked to be a baptism sponsor called the parish office. The grooms are getting married at another Catholic church; the man was asked to be a sponsor at his god-child's parish. They each need an affidavit stating that they are Catholic and a registered member of a parish faith community. Although all three stated that they attend Mass at this parish, and have for several years, none had ever registered. If they had been registered parishioners, there would have been no question or problem getting the necessary form. But they were not registered; they were unknown to the parish staff.

Registering in a parish is a declaration of your desire to be part of a Catholic community and to make a commitment to the life of the parish family. Clearly stating your Catholic commitment in all its dimensions brings many advantages, recognition, and responsibility.

Being a registered parishioner makes the process much easier when it is time for infant baptism, school registration, weddings, when asked to be a baptismal or confirmation sponsor, and even funerals. Registering as a parishioner also has some financial benefits: lower rates for school tuition, religious education charges, and wedding fees. A registered parishioner also receives all parish mailings. Church law advises that territories or boundaries no longer limit parish registration. We accept anyone who wants to share in the life of our parish regardless of where they live. Why not sign up today? Use the form inserted in the bulletin. You can also call Theresa Smith at 222-222-2222, or stop in at the parish office.

1.2. Why Register?

It is no coincidence that there is a common root in the etymology of the words "communion" and "community." As social beings, we humans need each other. We especially sense that a positive relationship emerges when we come together for prayer and worship. While there is a profusion of books and other resources on individual spirituality, prayer, and devotion, there is also an innate desire to be part of a larger faith community and not just develop one's spirituality in isolation.

Think back to any meetings you have attended, whether a church, school, or community meeting. Typically people are introduced or are asked to introduce themselves, or maybe a piece of paper is passed around asking people to sign in. The organization or organizers need that information for further contact and/or follow-up. The same is true of church congregations. Most of us belong to churches that have records going back years, decades—and in some cases, centuries. There is a need to maintain that data and collect new data. Let's start from the very beginning with a look at how to collect data about parishioners and what data should be collected.

1.3. Parish Census Form

There are many census forms available from parish information services, church publishers, and related companies. Some are meant to be entered into an electronic database; others are printed on a card stock and sized to fit nicely in a file cabinet. In today's electronic era with inexpensive computers and easy-to-use information programs, every parish can have instant access to a wealth of information that will help parish ministers better serve the needs of parishioners. Data cards are nice, but computer data records are so much better.

A sample confidential parish census form is printed in Appendix A. This may appear to be a very detailed form, but it gathers the data that is essential for a parish to operate effectively in many spiritual, social, and service areas. The appendix also contains instructions about how

to order copies of this form for parish use. With this and many similar forms available, there is little need for a parish to reinvent the wheel or start from scratch by developing its own form.

The remainder of this chapter suggests ways to utilize various elements of the standard parish census data that is gathered from this or similar forms.

1.4. Basic Name and Address

How can an organization exist if it doesn't even know who its members are? How can it serve its members if it doesn't know what they need or want? The most basic items needed for a parish census are the members' names and addresses. Once a parish has this minimal data it can begin to communicate with its members every day, not just on the Sundays that they attend services.

Announcements made at weekend liturgies and information printed in the parish's weekly bulletin do not reach the entire congregation. Did they ever? Considering everything from distractions at Mass to poor sound systems to readers who do not speak clearly to bulletins getting lost on the trip home, parishes need to expand their means of communication to their parishioners.

The basic parish mailing list can get the word out to all of its parishioners quickly and economically. This can be done through mailings informing members of special liturgies, invitations to social events, or maybe in a newsletter that provides a calendar of all upcoming activities, or an annual directory of parish information and activities. This information is also necessary if a parish mails its contribution envelopes. Using a non-profit bulk postage permit from the United States Postal Service makes it even more affordable.

1.5. Salutation

Many census programs include a field for the sender to note a personal salutation. This comes in quite handy when personalizing a letter to the whole congregation or to a specific group of members. It's a small thing, but many parishioners appreciate a letter that begins with *Dear Bob and Barbara* instead of *Dear Mr. and Mrs. Robert Donor* or worse yet, *Dear Parishioner*. It is not always practical to personalize every parish communication but it certainly makes a difference. Just take care to match the proper letter with the correct mailing label. An alternate approach is to hand-address an envelope for a personal touch. It is also practical to use a window envelope in which the inside address shows though and becomes the mailing address.

1.6. First Names

Obviously you need and want full names, not just initials. And you want this data from each family member. Having the individual family members' names in the parish database provides an opportunity to have a little fun with parish bulletin fillers.

Parish Saints

Most parishes publish a calendar of feast days for the coming week in the Sunday bulletin. At the end of the list wish a "Happy Feast Day" to the parishioners named after those saints. List the number of Margarets, Peters, or Polycarps living in the parish. You won't be able to list each woman named Monica, but you can mention that twenty-two Monicas celebrate with the great saint on her feast day of August 27.

To do this, have the parish database sort by alphabetical order the first names of all parishioners. Remember to take into consideration the variations on the names and the ethnic possibilities. When you count the number of men named John, you want to include and mention all the ones named Sean, Ian, Ivan, and Juan. And if your last name happens to be James or George, you deserve a mention, too, on the feast of those saints!

1.7. Male or Female

Steak fries, Super Bowl parties, craft sales, bowling leagues, beauty make-over nights, Good Friday men's choir, women's clubs—some events involve men and women, but other events are designed to keep the sexes apart. A parish database that can easily select a particular group (for example, married women over the age of forty) is extremely helpful.

Revitalizing a Parish Organization

At one parish the Altar and Rosary Society was dying a slow death, as women were no longer interested in getting involved in cleaning the altar or praying the rosary together. A few younger female parishioners re-formed the group into the Women's Club with a decidedly different focus on activities and fund-raising events. A major part of the revitalization came from personally inviting the women of the parish to become involved. Using the parish census data, it was easy to print mailing labels for the female members of the parish within a certain age range. The special mailing, along with bulletin announcements and word-of-mouth invitations generated by the existing members, had a tremendous effect. At the parish that did this 75 percent of the attendees at the next meeting had never before come to a women's club meeting. They came because of the personal invitation they received.

1.8. Date of Birth

Another vital piece of information along with a person's name is the individual's age. Age is a good filter for mailings. You don't want to invite a twelve-year-old to the women's club and it is unlikely that a senior citizen will want to play in the youth basketball league.

Use age data to make sure that children of the parish are being invited to receive religious instruction. Review the list of school-age children each September to make sure they are enrolled in either the school or religious education program. It can be amazing to see how many children fall through the cracks. Pass the information to the director of religious education, who can contact those families and invite them to enroll in the religious education program.

In the spring, review the list again as the school prepares for its annual "open house" for the coming school year. Provide the school with the names of the parents of all three- and four-year-old children. The school staff, in turn, can then invite them to a special open house for the preschool program.

Age Has Its Privileges

Like it or not, we all grow older. Sometimes reaching a certain age grants us more privileges. One of the ways a parish can use date-of-birth information is to send birthday cards. One parish sends birthday cards to everyone sixty-five and older. Several mail-order companies offer religious and scriptural cards that are positive and hopeful. Some even have a humorous twist. At one parish a stay-at-home mom has been the greeting card volunteer for several years. She gets a quarterly list of senior citizen birthdays and a supply of cards and stamps. Of course, should a parishioner die between the printing of the list and his or her birthday, a member of the parish staff makes a quick phone call advising the volunteer secretary in order to avoid any distress.

Throughout this manual there are suggestions about how to involve various segments of the parish population in events and activities when it is essential to be able to obtain a person's age from the parish database.

1.9. Sacraments Received

A listing of the sacraments that a person has received and when and where they have been received is another vital bit of parish data. This information can be used in many positive and productive ways. For example, this information is needed when registering children in the parish school or religious education program. Reviewing dates of baptism, First Communion, first reconciliation, and confirmation will provide lists of the people who have not received one or more of these sacraments and are in need of instruction or at least an invitation to instruction.

One archdiocese noted that many people now in their twenties or older had not been confirmed. The archdiocese began offering special instruction for these adults. Through the parish census database it is possible to locate numerous prospects. Some of the adults missed the opportunity to be confirmed as children due to a family move or family crisis. Others went through a period when they or their family did not attend church regularly.

It may also be the case that some of the records are incorrect or incomplete. In fact, a person may have been confirmed at another church or as part of a school program and the information was not added to the parish database. In some cases the records are kept in the huge leather-bound books of permanent parish records but not added to the individual profiles in the census program. Thus it is important that shortly after a parishioner is married or a baby is baptized or a person receives any sacrament, the records of the individual, family, and household are updated so that the parish database is as current as it can be.

1.10. Denomination

Parish census information should also address the many interfaith couples and families in the parish. Often a non-Catholic individual has been attending Mass with his or her spouse or family but has never received an invitation to consider the possibility of becoming a Catholic.

Evangelization Outreach

Review the list of the non-Catholic members of the parish and give this data to the Adult Initiation team. Contacting these people can generate many new inquirers. Even if the person is not interested in exploring the Christian initiation process at this time, it may be possible to conduct a few ecumenical services throughout the year. Not only will interfaith marriage families be recognized, but other Christians who live in the neighborhood but are not parishioners might attend. These occasional but well planned services might open a new stream of inquirers.

1.11. Marriage Date

While it is essential to record the dates when children receive the sacraments, it is also necessary to maintain data about which parishioners are married, when the marriage took place, and whether or not it was a ceremony recognized by the Catholic Church.

The record of marriage data coupled with the information about the death of parishioners can also allow a parish to reach out to a widow or widower on their wedding anniversary. Sending a card or even making a pastoral phone call to someone who has lost a loved one and has to mark a special wedding anniversary alone is another way to minister compassionately to individual members of the parish community.

Remembering parishioners' wedding anniversaries is yet another opportunity to extend a greeting to particular members of the parish congregation. Aside from remembering the couple with an anniversary card, special celebrations can be developed each year to celebrate the milestone anniversaries (twenty-five, forty, fifty, sixty years). While individual couples may have their own special anniversary celebration with or without a church service, having an annual event that honors couples married twenty-five, forty, fifty, or sixty years adds joy to their lives and reminds others of the sacred nature of the sacrament of marriage.

1.12. Date of Death

Keeping track of who has died and when they died is essential to providing grief ministry and support to loved ones and surviving relatives. A remembrance, a card, or a phone call one month, six months, and one year after a loved one has died is invaluable. Inviting family members and loved ones to a memorial event is another excellent pastoral initiative, made easier by having a database that easily provides such information. Conversely, addressing a parish notice or sending an annual giving statement to Mr. and Mrs. Jones when one of them has died in the past year can cause unnecessary pain.

1.13. Annual Celebrations

Having a record of the date of baptisms, weddings, deaths, graduations, and similar milestone events can make it easier to celebrate special anniversaries. It is an opportunity to give religious significance to an event that is either overlooked or celebrated solely in a secular manner.

Memorial Events

During the course of a year there are opportunities to commemorate as a parish all those who have celebrated a special event in the past year. The parish database provides the information of who needs to be contacted and how they can be reached.

• *January—Baptism of the Lord*: Parishes often celebrate individual infant baptisms at a time apart from the weekend parish liturgies. Invite all people (infants and adults) baptized in the previous year to a special celebration on the feast of the Baptism of the Lord. It is an opportunity for the parish to take hope from the many newly baptized members.

• *February—Valentine's Day:* Like baptisms, weddings are celebrated with family and friends present—out of sight of the parish members who attend the regular weekend liturgies. Invite all the couples married in the past twelve months to attend a special Mass, blessing, and renewal of vows. Hold the event at one (or more) of the parishes Masses on the weekend closest to Valentine's Day.

• *June—Graduation Day:* If the parish has a school, there are probably events recognizing the graduates of that institution. What about the other students of the parish graduating from other grammar or high schools or from college? The parish records should indicate who is likely to be graduating. Invite them all to come to a particular parish Mass one weekend, at which they will receive a special graduation blessing—and possibly a memento. Of course, it is also an opportunity to invite them to become more involved and share their newly acquired talents and education with the parish family.

- *November—All Souls:* The family members and friends of everyone who has been buried from the parish in the past twelve months should be invited to a commemorative Mass at which the names of all those who have died are read aloud and prayed for in a special way.

For each of these events, there can be a special memento, a reception afterwards, and other personal touches that make this an event to remember and a memory to cherish. The section on parish faith-building activities will offer more suggestions on how to make each event memorable.

1.14. Language

How many languages are spoken at your parish? Is it time to offer a Mass in Spanish or Polish or another language other than English? A review of parish census data, provided people have been given an opportunity to list their ethnic background and whether or not they speak other languages, might provide the data needed to consider offering Mass, other services, and sacraments in other languages. It also might indicate a need for instructional classes for both children and adults in other languages.

1.15. New Members

The parish database should indicate when a person joined the parish. Special effort should be made to welcome new members to events and remind them of the benefits and services available to them now that have joined the parish.

Welcoming Events

It is often a good idea to host a brunch or dinner welcoming new members. Depending on the number of parishioners who register, this can be a monthly or quarterly event. At the gathering, have parish members explain the events and activities that take place at the parish and invite them to participate and to become involved. More important than the type and amount of food is the spirit that is generated by welcoming, informing, and inviting.

New members should also receive personal invitations to parish events during their first year as members. While veteran parishioners understand what the parish block party, Lenten mission, or fish fry are all about, newcomers won't. Just like a person newly married into a family, they will need a little hand-holding and history-telling to make them feel comfortable.

Host Families

Consider asking a longtime parish member or parish family to adopt a new family. This might range from personally inviting the new members to parish events or having them over to dinner with other parish families to help break the ice. It is especially beneficial when the host family is a neighbor of the new family. To know who is a neighbor to whom, however, a parish needs a database that can be accessed by address as well as by name.

Of course, anything that is recommended for families is also recommended for singles. Not every new parishioner is part of a mother-father-son-daughter family unit. There are singles, married couples with no children, widows, extended families, blended families, stepfamilies, and every other imaginable type of family unit and couple grouping. The parish database can be helpful in noting these various situations.

1.16. Special Groups of Members

A parish is composed of many types of people united in a common faith but separated by age, sex, background, education, and level of participation—not to mention factors like race, ethnic origin, and socioeconomic status. Ideally a parish welcomes all people and makes an effort to bring them together in praise of the Lord and service to one another and the wider community. The parish database can be invaluable as the staff attempts to understand the diversity of the parish congregation. Several groups deserve special consideration.

• *Nursing Home Residents:* One way to review parish census data for errors or duplications is to sort by house number and street name. When more than one surname is listed at an address and it is more than a blended or intergenerational family, it may be an indication of a multifamily dwelling or apartment house. It can also be a nursing home or care center. If that is the case, the parish staff can arrange a variety of services. This can include bringing Communion to those who are unable to attend Mass and placing copies of weekly parish bulletins in the common areas. The bulletin also provides a way for visitors to the nursing home to know that there is a nearby church that they can attend.

• *Distant Parishioners:* While most parishioners live within what are generally termed "the parish boundaries," a search of ZIP codes in the database will reveal which registered parishioners are traveling past other churches to get to the church where they are registered. They are making this special effort for a reason. Whether it is returning to the church of one's youth or consciously choosing this church because of its liturgies and services, these parishioners need to feel that they are part of the church and community even though they don't live in the proximate geographic community.

• *Unregistered Parishioners:* Take special note of the loose checks in the basket when the weekend collection is counted. To ensure that the donor receives credit for their donation, match the loose check with the parish directory. It might just be someone who forgot to use the collection envelope. It is likely, however, that there are donations from non-registered parishioners who live within the parish boundaries. This can be a source of new members.

1.17. Occupation and Skills

Parishioners come to church on the weekend. What do they do from Monday to Friday? Can this skill or talent, or some hobby or personal interest, be of value to the parish? Likewise, what can a parish do to meet the needs of these people?

Knowing the educational background and profession of parishioners can guide the adult formation program directors to target programs to the needs of special groups within the parish. There can be career counseling, peer mentoring, or a special reflection night for those in a particular profession.

When the parish or an individual parishioner is looking for a good contractor or a medical or service professional, it is often more reliable to look through a list of parishioners than the telephone book! The parish census can include a skills list, asking members to volunteer for gardening, painting, decorating, tutoring, or many other parish activities.

The parish census can also offer a checklist of skills and ministries that allows registrants to check a specific ministry they want to learn more about and a list of skills they possess. In this way, staff members can recruit volunteers for specific needs in their ministry. For example, imagine having a list of people who list typing as a skill. They may be asked to help with some volunteer office duty. Those who check carpentry might be called on for simple repairs around the parish or to help build a stage or backdrops for the school play. Many churches offer funeral lunches by calling on those who noted on their census form an interest in cooking or food service.

> ### Parish University
>
> One parish, after completing its census and collecting the occupational data, opened a parish "university." The "university" offers classes taught by volunteers. The participants pay a fee for the class and the fees support the scholarship program of the school. The volunteers donate their time. By knowing an individual's occupation and skills it was possible to offer a range of programs as diverse as knitting, calligraphy, Spanish language, cooking, and aerobics. Some classes might last for one session only while others might run for several meetings.

1.18. Make the Post Office Happy

By reviewing your census data on an annual basis you can catch spelling and other errors. Try sorting by street name. You can then scan the list for consistency, making sure that all street names are spelled correctly each and every time. It is also a good time to review postal recommendations and regulations regarding punctuation and abbreviations. Determine if proper usage calls for "North Riverside" or "N. Riverside," "Forest Park" or "Forest Pk." Correcting the data keeps the postal workers happy and hopefully gets the mail delivered in a timely fashion.

1.19. Privacy

The information parishioners provide in their census registration is extremely personal. As such, it must be stated clearly on the form and on any and all letters of introduction or notices regarding the census form that their data is held in strictest confidence and shared with no one outside the parish staff. Make it clear that the parish staff will only use the information for parish business, and that no unauthorized use of this data will be tolerated.

If the diocese or a specific religious organization or group asks to use the mailing list, it is best to decline. You may, however, want to offer to mail their materials for them, thereby protecting your promise of privacy to your parishioners. In those cases, the group requesting the mailing should pay all costs, including the time it takes the staff to label the mailing. And if the parish list is used for such a mailing, it is a good idea to mention this in the bulletin. Advise parishioners that the mailing was made under the auspices of the parish, but the outside group did not have access to the parish records.

Conclusion

Developing and maintaining a parish census database is a major undertaking. Once it is completed, there is no limit to the ways it can be used to improve the organization of the parish and expand its outreach. The suggestions provided here are just a beginning. Throughout this manual there will be many other references to the parish database as the primary key to developing the parish.

Financial Information:
The Key to Funding Your Parish

Parishes cannot exist without the financial support of generous parishioners and guests who attend services or fund-raising activities. As stewards of the parish, business managers and other parish administrators have an obligation to make sure that a sufficient amount of money is collected and then spent wisely.

For their part, parishioners have an obligation to support the parish financially along with sharing their time and talent. The parish administration, however, needs to report regularly on the financial health (or illness) of the parish to the entire congregation, and to present in an informative and appealing way the financial needs of the parish to its members. People have to be asked, encouraged, told, and reminded to give and to give generously.

There are several practical steps that the parish staff can take to monitor, encourage, and increase donations. It starts with wise use of the parish database and incorporates other ideas that lead to a total stewardship program.

2.1. Collection Envelopes

Make giving an easy process. Use an envelope company to mail contribution envelopes to all parishioners. While some parishes set up tables at the beginning of the year with an entire box of envelopes for the whole year for each parishioner, it is generally more effective to mail contribution envelopes on a monthly, bimonthly, or quarterly basis. Too often those annual envelope boxes get lost in some drawer at home.

Sending a periodic supply of envelopes provides a timely reminder of the need for church support. If a special appeal is planned, an extra envelope can be inserted on short notice. The ability to update parish address lists at any time is another reason for sending envelopes throughout the year.

Since the envelope supplier works with many parishes, the company representative will have advice on how other churches manage their program or design their envelopes.

2.2. Recording Contributions

There are excellent, easy-to-use software packages for recording contributions. It allows for efficient and accurate record-keeping of weekend and special donations. It also allows for customized thank-you letters.

Linking such a program to the parish database is a must. The days of having the teenager who answers the phone in the evening kept busy by recording weekly donations on an index card are over.

Remember to record the contributions of people who regularly use a check but not an envelope.

2.3. Locating Unknown Donors

You can look for unknown donors in the same place you looked for unregistered parishioners—the collection basket. Take note of the loose checks collected each week, and try to match the checks with names and addresses in the parish directory. Every week there are likely to be donations from unregistered people who live within the parish boundaries.

Begin by recording this new census information on a simple index card. If an unregistered parishioner makes additional donations, record them on the card. Once a month, review the cards, send a thank-you note, and encourage them to consider joining the parish. When they do register, transfer their donation history from the card to the census contribution program in the parish database.

Another way to uncover unknown parishioners is through analysis of personal checks used to pay for things like choir CDs, women's club cookbooks, or similar items like "stock certificates" that fund the youth club. Recording these purchases just like un-enveloped checks in the weekend collection indicates the unregistered members of the congregation. It gives another opportunity to invite them to become part of the parish family of God.

2.4. Seasonal Collection Letters

Envelope mailing companies can also handle the mailing of Christmas and Easter letters. Avoid having the burden of printing, copying, folding, stuffing, sealing, addressing, and mailing hundreds or thousands of letters fall to the parish staff or a cadre of volunteers. Let the envelope company send the seasonal mailing. Combine a letter from the pastor with a holy day service schedule and a special appeal envelope.

The pastor's letter should contain a spiritual message and an invitation to attend the liturgical celebrations. Either in his letter or in an additional letter, there should be an appeal for a special contribution. Include a chart of last year's donations as a gentle reminder of the different levels of generosity. Educate parishioners to the realization that the goal for the special Christmas and Easter collections is four to six times the regular Sunday amount—if that is the case. Telling them what the parish needs allows the parishioners to respond appropriately.

2.5. Sample Letter and Giving Chart

Dear Parishioners and Friends:

Several months ago, I was privileged to present at Mass and in the parish newsletter the annual report on both parish ministries and finances. Even before I spoke, I think you knew it was going to be good news. You knew the results because you made it happen! Your generous sharing of your time, talent, and treasure makes it possible for our community to support the more than fifty ministries that make our parish a great place to be.

At Christmas time, we hear so many wonderful stories about gift giving. O. Henry's story *The Gift of the Magi* teaches us about gifts of sacrifice. What sacrifice are we willing to make this Christmas?

The story of the Three Kings presenting Jesus with gifts of gold, frankincense, and myrrh teaches us about giving appropriate gifts. Many of us spend a considerable amount of time and money selecting the perfect Christmas presents for family and friends. We try to make sure each gift will be special for that particular person. Sometimes, on Christmas Eve, we find ourselves struggling to get everything wrapped or heading out to purchase one more gift certificate. This Christmas, as you reflect, plan, make notes, or whatever you do before heading out to start your Christmas shopping, I ask you to consider using some of the same time to consider your appropriate sacrifice and gift to your parish.

Our Christmas goal this year is $100,000—just slightly more than what you so generously contributed last year. For your reference, I have listed the details of last year's Christmas collection. With your prayerful consideration, I am sure that together we will meet our goal.

In gratitude,

Name
Parish Business Manager

Gift Amount	No. of Gifts		Gift Amount	No. of Gifts
$7,500, $6,000, $5,000	1 each		$200-$299	39
$3,800, $2,000	1 each		$100-$199	195
$1,500, $1,000	2 each		$75-$99	26
$800, $700	1 each		$50-$74	169
$500	19		$25-$49	175
$400	2		$10-$24	109
$300-$399	14		Up to $10	23

2.6. Increased Donation Campaigns

Some parishes employ a development consulting firm to conduct a complex, multifaceted program to increase donations, or to mobilize the entire parish for a capital campaign to construct a new building or refurbish an existing one. These programs that utilize outside consultants are often necessary and can bring people to a deeper awareness of stewardship and a higher level of giving.

On the other hand, there are simpler and less complicated ways to increase donations. Happy parishioners are often the best givers. People are willing to pay for good service. If the congregation feels welcome and well served, their giving will reflect those feelings. If they are encouraged to become involved in many ways and share their talent through volunteer work, they will become part of the active parish community and not just be a bystander or "pew potato."

If there is a capital campaign with pledges to be fulfilled over a period of months or years, it is important to use the parish database to send out reminders to those who made a pledge. Provide them with a list of their contributions and the schedule that they agreed to meet. It is amazing to see how donations increase when folks realize that they have fallen behind in their contributions. At the same time other letters can be sent to thank everyone who is making contributions to the campaign according to their pledge. Another letter can be prepared for those parishioners who either have not contributed or have not pledged to the parish campaign.

Of course, while the database can provide the necessary categories of people, it is the staff's responsibility to see that the proper letter is sent to each person.

Besides special giving campaigns and a general effort to serve parishioners in a way that will cause them to respond generously, there are times when congregations need to be reminded of special needs or basic operating budget concerns. Use the parish database to see what people have given before. Ask them to meet or exceed that goal.

2.7. Target Likely Donors

A parish can better target fund-raising events by using the database of donations as a filter. For example, a parish may have an annual raffle for which tickets are $100 each. There also might be a dinner dance at $75 per person. Yet another fund-raiser might seek donors to sponsor or subsidize a student's tuition charges. A parish could waste a lot of money sending raffle tickets, invitations, and brochures to parishioners who contributed a total of less than $100 in the previous year. It is unlikely that they will purchase a $100 raffle ticket if they didn't even contribute $2 per week in the collection basket.

Advertise these events in the weekly bulletin to keep all parishioners informed and offer everyone a way to obtain tickets, but target the special appeals to the most likely donors. It decreases the mailing and printing costs and thereby increases the profit.

2.8. Adding New Donors

One parish that began a capital campaign noticed that it had received many donations from families that had not initially pledged to participate in the campaign. Although they had not pledged a set amount or used the signup forms, they began to use the envelopes. These contributions were recorded and an analysis of the data gave the parish business staff an opportunity to request a formal pledge from them. This had the potential to increase their donation.

2.9. Alumni Donors

As parishioners move out of the parish, don't hit the delete key too quickly. Just as families and schools host reunions, so do parishes. We know them, however, as golden jubilee celebrations or annual dinner dances.

Create a separate file for former parishioners and use it to invite people to special parish events. An annual newsletter to the parish alums can serve as a vehicle to keep them informed about the parish. The parish alumni association also has the potential to become part of the base of financial support through an annual appeal or through designated giving at anniversary events.

If the parish does not have such a database of former parishioners, ask current parishioners to provide the names and addresses of friends, relatives, and neighbors who once lived in the parish. If the school has an alumni association for graduates, place a notice in the alumni association newsletter or fund-raising appeal asking the graduates to provide their parents' and siblings' addresses.

2.10. Annual Statements

To send annual statements to every donor or not: that is the question. The parish staff needs to decide if donation summary statements should be sent to all donors, to all parishioners regardless of whether or not they donated anything, only to those who contribute more than a certain amount, or only those who specifically ask for a statement.

Consider placing a notice in the weekly bulletin during January indicating that contribution statements will be mailed only to those who request them. One parish that sent statements to everyone for years found out that less that 10 percent of envelope users really wanted or needed a statement. Many apparently kept track for

themselves and many others did not itemize their deductions on their taxes so the statement was not necessary.

On the other hand sending a statement allows the parish staff to remind people of the expectations and needs of the parish. It might be a good idea to send a contribution statement to every family that has a child in the school or religious education program. It provides an opportunity to remind parents of the fact that the parish subsidizes their child's education by X percent or X dollars each year—and why it is so important for them to support the parish financially.

2.11. Reminder Notices

Consider sending a contribution statement after the end of the third quarter (current as of September 30) in the months before the year ends. Include a reminder notice advising them that if they missed a Sunday or two, now would be the perfect time to catch up with their weekly commitment to the parish.

Since this is an opportunity to solicit contributions, consider sending the third-quarter statement to the entire parish membership. It is a legitimate hope that they will evaluate their giving before the end of the year and help the parish with increased donations to reach its budgeted income before the end of the year.

2.12. Sample Reminder Letter

This letter can be sent to all parishioners along with their third-quarter statement. It can also be adjusted so that it can be sent near the end of the fiscal year. If the fiscal year ends on June 30, send a revised version of this letter in mid-May.

Dear Parishioner:

As we approach the end of the year, I have enclosed a contribution statement for all donations made between January 1 and September 30. Please review your statement and report any discrepancies to the parish office.

As reported in the weekly bulletin, we are running a slight deficit in our budgeted Sunday offering. The Sunday offering is the largest source of income for our parish. We are grateful that higher-than-expected Christmas and Easter collections and a concerted effort by staff members to reduce expenses will help mitigate the Sunday shortfall. However, deferring expenses is not a long-term solution.

I hope that if you find you missed making a Sunday or Easter contribution, you will become current with your donations before December 31. For your convenience, a self-addressed envelope is included in your packet of contribution envelopes.

The Sunday offering goal for the current year is $00,000 per week. Our average Sunday offering for this year has been $00,000. We need to increase our offering by $0,000 per week to meet our budget. Please remember your commitment to the parish and, if possible, increase your weekly contribution. If you received a raise in your salary or pension, consider increasing your contribution to the church by the same percentage.

Lastly, thank you for your support throughout the year. With over 000 volunteers serving the mission of our parish, nearly 0,000 people praying as a community at church each weekend, and the financial support of so many longtime and new parishioners, we look forward to continuing to serve the spiritual, social, and service needs of our parishioners.

Wishing you every blessing for your generosity,

Name
Parish Business Manager

2.13. Converting Non-contributors

The number of households that do not make any financial contributions in the course of a year or many years can be staggering. One wonders if they have moved, do not attend church regularly, are in financial difficulty, or are among the innumerable churchgoers who neatly fold and drop a single dollar bill into the collection basket. When their parents and grandparents did that, a dollar bought something. Today, while every dollar in the collection counts, it is hard to imagine that someone cannot afford to contribute more.

Review the list and note any hardship cases that should not receive a notice. Then prepare to contact all the non-contributors to find out if they wish to remain parishioners or if they are unable to attend church and need a home visit by a parish minister of care.

This might be the time to use a postcard. A personal phone call or visit may be too intrusive, a letter might not get opened. If they have not responded to any previous appeals or parish invitations, they are probably "recycling" anything that has the parish return address on it.

The text of the postcard could read:

We haven't heard from you in a while . . . and we miss you!

We need your presence at our liturgies as we praise God and pray for the cares of the world. We hope you need us, too. We also need your generosity to accomplish what our church is all about: good liturgy, excellent education for children and adults, responsible youth ministry, and conscious social action. Our records indicate that you have not used your church contribution envelopes in over X years. If this is incorrect, please let us know.

If you wish to remain a member of _____ Parish and enjoy all of the benefits of parishioner status, please return this postcard in the Sunday offering basket or mail it to the parish office by _____. If we do not hear from you, we will update our records.

☐ Yes, I wish to remain a registered parishioner of _____ Church.

☐ I have special needs. Please have a minister of care contact me. My phone number is _____

One parish that sent this notice to three hundred members received fifty responses asking to remain as parishioners. Another ten people asked to be contacted by a minister of care. The parish sent a follow-up personalized letter to those who did respond to the postcard in an envelope with a fluorescent yellow sticker asking for their immediate reply. The text of the letter read:

Dear «NAME»:

On (date), _____ Parish mailed a postcard to 000 parishioners, you included, who had not used a contribution envelope in over three years. Unfortunately, there is no way, except through a contribution analysis, to determine if our parishioners are actively involved in the parish, as we do not have a means of taking attendance on Sundays.

We asked that you return the postcard if you wished to remain a parishioner of _____ Church. We have heard from several people who have asked us not to terminate their parishioner status. They indicated that they were unable to contribute until their current financial situation changed. We were glad to hear from them and are happy to leave them enrolled; we pray for their needs.

Please understand that it is not necessary to make financial contributions to maintain your parish registration; but as you know, the parish cannot maintain our high level of ministries and programs without the active participation and financial support of our parishioners.

Perhaps you registered in the parish many years ago in order to be married, have your child baptized, or to enroll your child in the parish school or the religious education program. In the meantime, maybe you have found another faith community.

By this letter, we are only asking that you assist us in carrying out Jesus' ministry by completing the short survey on the reverse side. Please use the enclosed envelope to return your completed survey. As we work together to fulfill God's covenant, the staff at _____ Parish thanks you for your time in responding to our request.

Please call the parish office at 222-222-2222 if you would like to speak with me or another member of the parish staff. Our goal is to serve you by bringing you closer to Christ.

Sincerely,

Name
Parish Business Manager

The back side asked for their feedback:

I attend Mass regularly at _____ Parish. Please keep my name active in the parish registry.
❏ Yes
❏ No

I currently attend another church.
❏ Yes, I attend _____
❏ No

I am unable to attend Mass and wish to have a minister of care bring Communion to my home.
❏ Yes, please have a minister of care contact me.
My phone number is _____

I no longer attend the parish because:

My constructive suggestions to improve the parish are (please indicate whether you would be willing to volunteer to help make these changes):

(Please use as much space as needed or attach another sheet. Please be sure to include your name in case we have any questions and need to contact you.)

Included with the letter was a self-addressed return envelope. The parish that used this follow-up letter received another fifty responses. Many were in fact attending other Catholic churches. At this point the 170 households that did not respond were placed in an inactive status. They have not yet been deleted from the parish database or census program but they have been removed from the active mailing list. Should they come to the church requesting one of the sacraments, this information would be easily accessed and would be a factor in the pastoral care that is offered.

Conclusion

The less a pastor or parish business manager or administrator has to say about money the better. Good financial programs, effectively managed, can be nearly invisible. The parish database and the information about contribution records allow for a parish giving program that is precise, direct, unobtrusive, and successful.

Parish Survey:
The Key to Understanding Your Parish

What makes someone register at a particular church? Why do longtime parishioners stay at a parish? What do people like or dislike about a parish? What services do they wish the parish provided? A parish survey can answer these and many other questions.

Geography is a big answer to why people register at a particular parish, but this factor is not as important as it once was. People are willing to drive a distance, especially in a city or town with several parishes, to find the quality and tone of services they prefer.

A parish survey can reveal other interesting information. What attracted them to the church? How long had they been attending services before they actually registered? What might be lacking? Addressing those issues might enable a parish to attract more people for whom that particular issue, service, or activity is very important.

3.1. New Member Survey

Here is a sample questionnaire that can be used with new members. Send it out once a year to everyone who has registered in the past twelve months.

New Parishioner Survey

We are privileged and honored that you have chosen to become a member of this parish in the past year. We would like to learn more about your decision to join us. Please take a few minutes to complete the enclosed questionnaire. This will help us better understand your decision process and ultimately tell us how we can reach out to other members of the parish family. Please return the survey by the end of the month. Mail it or drop it in the Sunday collection basket. A return envelope is enclosed for your convenience.

How long have you lived in the area? _____ years _____ months

How did you first hear about this parish?

What prompted you to begin attending Mass here?

How long did you attend Mass at this parish before you formally registered?

In joining this parish, what do you hope to experience?

Aside from Sunday Mass, what other events or church functions did you attend before registering as a parishioner?

Before registering at this parish, were you a member of another church (of another faith)? _____ If yes, which one?

What prompted you to leave that parish and seek another parish?

What are your interests in the community? (Check all that apply.)
- ❑ Liturgical Ministry (lector, Communion minister, usher, choir member)
  Which ones? _____

- ❑ Spiritual (Bible class, small-group study, Book-of-the-Month)
  Which ones? _____

- ❑ Social Ministry (food pantry, visiting homebound, sister parish service)
  Which ones? _____

- ❑ Education (catechist, youth minister, adult education)
  Which ones? _____
  What age level?_____

In your opinion, what is the parish known for?

Based on your observations, what are the strengths of this parish?

How would you like to learn about the parish's events?
❑ Parish bulletin
❑ E-mail
❑ Mailed newsletter
❑ Telephone
❑ Sunday announcements
❑ Signs at church entryway

On a scale of 1–5 (1 indicating the lowest score, 5 indicating the highest score), how would you rate the parish and its services and members?

_____   Parishioners are approachable and friendly.
_____   Staff members are helpful and inviting.
_____   Parishioners and staff are eager to embrace newcomers.
_____   Communication about programs and events is clear and timely.
_____   Groups and programs exist that have my interest.
_____   The parish is spiritually satisfying and fulfilling.

What programs, events, ministries would you like to see this parish consider?

Please add any other comments.

Thank you very much for your input!

Optional Information:

Name: _____

_____

Address:_____

_____

Phone: (Home) _____ (Work) _____

E-mail: _____

_____

Thank you for completing this survey. It will benefit the parish staff and community as we learn more about what we do well and where we could improve.

3.2. Demographic Profile

Producers of goods and services must know who their customers are in order to provide the correct product. A store in Alaska generally does not carry Hawaiian shirts among its souvenirs. The same is true in a parish setting. The most effective parishes are the ones that offer programs and services that meet the needs of the congregation. If a program is not as well utilized or supported as might have been hoped, one possibility is that there are just not enough people in the congregation to support it. Programs that exist because "we've always done this" may no longer serve the needs of the present parish population.

A demographic profile or survey of the parishioners can help a parish staff to know what programs no longer serve the current membership. Keeping an outdated or outmoded program alive follows the "dead horse" model. The horse looks dead but the veterinarians realize that maybe if they begin some IV fluids and antibiotics it will come back to life. The architects construct a frame to support the horse upright. The beauticians apply make-up to improve the horse's color. Sometimes, someone has to be bold enough to say, "This horse is dead. Bury it."

The richest, most well organized parish cannot do everything. As parish resources become strained, it is imperative to ensure that the time and energy put forth are used wisely. At the same time, a survey of parish demographics may reveal untapped segments of the parish population. Reaching that untapped segment has the potential to breathe new life into the parish community and attract new members.

The parish database should provide the information needed for this demographic profile. If the database is not complete, a demographic survey of membership filled out as an addition to the current census form will provide the necessary information.

3.3. Demographic Worksheet

This worksheet will give you a bird's-eye view of your parish. After looking at the profile, look at the programs and ministries offered by your parish and determine if there are any segments that are underserved. Once you have completed this worksheet, the entire parish staff and parish council should review it. Get out the huge flip chart and start understanding who is in your parish. If you have a college or university nearby, you might also invite a marketing professor to offer some guidance.

The data from the new-member survey combined with the parish demographic data should present a clear picture of the people in the parish and many of their basic sacramental, spiritual, social, and service needs.

Total number of households ___

Total number of parishioners ___

Total number of adult parishioners
  (age 21+) ___

Total number of men (age 21+) ___

Total number of women (age 21+) ___

Average age of adult parishioners
  (age 21+) ___

Men age 65+ ___

Women age 65+ ___

Men age 45–64 ___

Women age 45–64 ___

Men age 25–44 ___

Women age 25–44 ___

Number of parishioners married ___

Number of parishioners divorced ___

Number of parishioners single ___

Number of parishioners widowed ___

Number of non-Catholic spouses ___

Number of parishioners not baptized

  ___

Number of parishioners not confirmed

  ___

Total number of non-adult parishioners
  (under age 21) ___

Number of school-age children
  (grades K–8) ___

Number of children under age 5 ___

Number of children in parish day
  school ___

Number of children in religious
  education program ___

Number of children not in either
  program ___

Number of high school–age youth ___

Ethnic composition of parish:

_____
_____
_____
_____
_____
_____
_____
_____
_____
_____

Communication:
The Key to Explaining Your Parish

The manner in which the weekend liturgies are celebrated and the content and delivery of the homily are the prime means of communicating the faith to the parishioners. They are not, however, the focus of this book.

There are many other important, essential, and valuable ways to spread the message about the parish and its activities, programs, and services. All of these efforts to communicate should have a common theme, style, tone, and approach. Parishes can learn the importance of branding from the major corporations. Logo, ink color, typeface, and tag line/slogan do matter. Call on parishioners with marketing, publicity, promotion, and direct-mail backgrounds to assist the parish staff in developing a unified, dignified, proper print image.

Once a parish has a brand image, logo, and the other details that accompany it, there are a number of places and ways to use it in explaining the mission, goals, activities, and services of the parish. The suggestions listed here are some of the basic forms of communication. There are many others that a parish can use.

4.1. Parish Directory

Helping parishioners stay in touch with each other through the use of an annual parish directory is a great use of parish data. Several companies specialize in composing and printing parish directories. (Other companies specialize in pictorial directories, which are explained next.)

The typical directory lists each parishioner's name, address, and phone number. There is also room for listing all staff members, parish council members, and the parish mission statement. Additional pages allow for a description of parish ministries, committees, and volunteer chairpersons. Organizing the last bit of data might show that the parish is lacking a ministry to a particular segment of your congregation. Be sure to list basic parish policies, such as how to secure parish facilities for group meetings and events or private gatherings. Explain the sacramental preparation procedure so that everyone knows the expectations for baptisms and weddings. Remember to include the information for funerals and anniversary celebrations.

If it is an annual directory, include a calendar of parish events for the entire year. It is also a good idea to provide a listing of local government phone numbers and frequently requested (arch)diocesan phone numbers and Web sites.

Whether the parish organizes the directory on its own or uses a local printer or a firm that specializes in parish directories, someone should solicit advertising to appear in the directory. This is what pays for the printing and distribution of the book.

To make sure the information in the directory is current, send a notice to everyone in the parish showing how their name, address, and phone number will appear in the directory. Offer the chance to have them list an e-mail address. Advise them to contact the parish office if they do not want their name, address, or phone number included in the directory. Some will want no listing; others will want just their name or name and address, without a phone number or e-mail address.

At the same time parishioners are contacted to verify address information, invite them to advertise their business in the directory. Most parishioners find it valuable to have a listing of business and professional people from the parish whom they can call upon for services.

4.2. Pictorial Directory

For a pictorial directory each parishioner, couple, or family sits for a portrait-quality photograph taken by the company producing the directory. A directory of photographs plus information is given to each parishioner. The pictorial directory also contains photos of the parish staff members and may include photos taken at activities and events conducted by the parish.

Just like the non-pictorial directory, there is a listing of parishioners' names and addresses, parish organizations and leaders, and space for advertising. Because pictorial directories are not usually annual undertakings, they generally do not contain a calendar of events.

These directories are ordinarily free to the parish. The cost is subsidized by the advertisers and by the people who are encouraged to purchase additional copies of their photos. The families and individuals are solicited to purchase the photographs for their homes or to distribute to their extended families just like graduation pictures. While they do not have to purchase the photographs, many will. Most of the parish directory companies are reputable, but check out references and the cost to parishioners of additional photos. Ultimately, nothing is free, so check out the costs ahead of time.

A pictorial directory can be a great resource

for both parishioners and staff. How often does someone in the parish community die and people don't know who they are? Consider posting the funeral arrangements (or a notice of the person's death if the funeral already took place during the week) at all of the church entrances. Clip their picture from the directory and affix it to the posted notice. Often people remember the face but not always the name.

Photo directories are also a great way for parishioners to get to know one another. People see someone at church or at a parish event but don't introduce themselves. They go home, find the person in the directory, and speak to them by name the next time they are together.

4.3. Parish Newsletter

The parish bulletin can be a source of information for those who attend Mass. A semiannual, quarterly, or monthly newsletter sent to households through the mail is another way to reach parishioners—those who attend Mass and those who do not, weekly communicants, the homebound, those who attend just at Christmas and Easter, and those who registered years ago but rarely use the services or programs of the parish.

Start small and build. Aim for three newsletters a year: September—the welcome back to school and start of activities issue; January—details on what has been happening and what programs are planned for the Lenten season; and June—the annual recap of events and plans for the summer. One issue should also include the annual financial and ministerial report for the fiscal year.

After the newsletter is mailed, place a notice in the bulletin announcing that the newsletter has been mailed and that every registered household should have received a copy. Since many people think they are registered just because they attend Mass, end the notice by asking people who have not received the newsletter to contact the parish office to make sure the parish has their correct address. Print this notice in the weekly bulletin for four consecutive weeks. Each time, a handful of people will call who thought they were registered but in fact were not. Others will have moved and forgotten to report their change of address. This is a great opportunity to help them register or update their information in the parish database.

4.4. Church Calendars

Church calendars are an effective way to keep the church present in every home. Many companies produce calendars with religious artwork. Some combine nature themes with scripture quotations or stewardship messages. Others focus on vocations to the priesthood and religious life. They also list the calendar of saints, holy days, and days of Lenten fasting.

Most calendars provide the local church with a prominent place to list important parish telephone numbers and perhaps the Mass schedule. The calendar most likely will include space for the local funeral home to advertise its services. The fee it pays underwrites the cost of the calendar. Thus, there is absolutely no cost to the parish! Church calendars are not the exclusive domain of the local undertaker. You might also consider asking a local car dealer, restaurant, or grocery store to participate in the calendar in exchange for their advertisements.

The parish calendar can provide a means for catechesis. As people turn the page month after month and read the listing of feast days, the parish bulletin, newsletter, or Web site can include a brief biography of the coming month's major saints.

Few parishes have the resources to produce their own distinct calendar. Parishes can, without great expense, personalize the preprinted calendar. When the typical funeral home calendar is distributed in December, distribute an insert listing all the parish events for the entire year. The household can keep the list attached to the calendar or write those parish events that they consider important to them on the main calendar. A school parent might want to note all the school board meetings. If the parish has a set schedule for meetings—choir practice is every Wednesday night, the liturgy committee meets the second Tuesday of each month, the book club meets the fourth Thursday of each month—these events could be noted as well on the insert.

By providing people with the dates of the major annual events in advance (parish anniversaries, fall festivals, dinner dances, etc.) people can note these events on their calendar at the start of the year before they make other plans. Of course, being able to provide such a list requires the parish staff and organization chairpersons to start planning early—sometimes as much as eighteen months ahead of an event. This might seem a daunting task at the first attempt but will undoubtedly prove invaluable each year. Besides, most events follow an annual calendar; it just takes that first step of sitting everyone down in front of the calendar and cooperating.

If the staff and volunteers are really ambitious, they can create a sheet of preprinted labels or stickers for households to affix to the calendar. A group of volunteers could also gather to mark the dates before the calendars are distributed. Consider noting just one parish event per month that would require a sticker. Colored stickers would really make the events stand out and draw attention.

4.5. Electronic Communications

Technology has allowed parishioners to have more than one address: a house address and an e-mail address. It's possible that the e-mail address is the best way to reach some people. When people sort through their regular mail they often divide it into three piles: open immediately, open later, recycle immediately.

E-mail is a little different. In most cases, people only give their e-mail address to people they know. When people check their e-mail inbox, they will quickly delete the spam. But then folks probably read most of the e-mail they receive from people they know.

If a parish intends to use e-mail as a means of communication, ask parishioners to e-mail their address to the parish e-mailbox. This request can be made in the bulletin or parish newsletter or through a note inserted by the contribution envelope company with a packet of envelopes. Occasionally place reminder announcements in the weekly bulletin so that others may join the "program" simply by e-mailing their address to the parish. By asking people to e-mail their address to the parish office, there is no need to key the data into an address book, thereby eliminating any typing errors; it is a simple copy-and-paste. E-mail addresses can be collected as part of the parish registration form and at the time parents register their children for school or religious education programs.

When sending the e-newsletter to hundreds of parishioners at once, the parish office staff may have to check with the Internet service provider so that the mass mailings go through and are not filtered out by the service provider as spam.

Consider sending a monthly update of parish events via e-mail. It is a fast and economical way to communicate. Within two months, one parish had over 10 percent of its parishioners requesting a monthly e-newsletter. A year later 20 percent were receiving the e-mails, and the response from the parishioners receiving the updates was terrific.

4.6. Parish Web Site

In addition to communicating to parishioners via e-mail, many parishes have developed Web sites. A Web site can offer up-to-the-minute information for parishioners and non-parishioners and can also offer archival information. The parish Internet presence has the opportunity to present Web surfers and electronic browsers with more information than could ever be disseminated in a new-parishioner orientation meeting or a parish bulletin or newsletter.

Because the Web surfer can access the parish Web site at any time and for any length of time, it is a good idea to include a great deal of information. Arrange it in a manner that allows for easy navigation. Start with the information included in the weekly parish bulletin or newsletter. The Web site should include a letter from the pastor or administrator, a page for school news, another page on worship and liturgy along with the schedule of Masses and services, yet another for upcoming social events, and maybe even a page for local community events.

The Web site can take on the same format and have the same look as the parish bulletin

and newsletter and other print communication, but it can be much more dramatic using photos, full color, and links to other Web sites in the parish or diocese or at a national level. Web sites can be developed by parish staff, volunteers, Internet service providers, or general Web hosting companies. Some bulletin printers, religious publishers, and religious Web hosting companies offer Web site development and Web site hosting specialized for parishes.

4.7. Web Site Content

This basic information should appear on the parish Web site:

1. Welcome letter from the pastor or administrator
2. Parish mission statement
3. Mass and prayer schedule
4. Listing of staff members/parish directory
5. Listing of upcoming events
6. Description of parish ministries
7. School/religious education programs and staff
8. Sacrament preparation procedures
9. Map of how to get to the church
10. History of the parish
11. Archive of previous parish bulletins and newsletters
12. Links to other Catholic Web sites—(arch)diocese, Vatican, Catholic Charities, religious orders that serve (or served) the parish, and local governmental agencies
13. Don't forget the spiritual aspect of parish life. Consider a prayer heading for each page of the Web site or a prayer for each day.
14. Sunday homilies—if they are available in text or audio format

4.8. Parish Phone System

Phone etiquette is a dying art. With automated voice mail systems, people and parishes are losing that personal touch in deference to efficiency. With the record volume of calls asking for Mass times just before Christmas, Ash Wednesday, or Easter, it might be necessary to use an automated system on busy days like this.

A call to a parish office should not involve a trip through voice mail hell, but answering the phone "live" presents other problems. It is hard to describe the various vocal tones on paper, but use your imagination for a minute.

"Hello?"

"OUR LADY OF MERCY!"

"Good morning, Our Lady of Mercy; this is Joan."

"G'morningSt.John's."

Care must also be taken when the caller actually speaks with a real person. Is the person answering the phone welcoming, friendly, knowledgeable? Does he or she speak in a clear, friendly tone that can be easily understood? Does a call to request information about scheduling a baptism turn into a mini-inquisition? Questions like "Are you a parishioner?" "Are you registered?" "Do you use envelopes?" can sound threatening to a person calling the church for the first time.

Keep a copy of the parish directory at the receptionist's desk. When the caller begins by stating that they have just become engaged or had a baby, saying something simple like "Congratulations!" can go a long way toward making them feel welcome and comfortable at the church. As the receptionist or parish staff member asks for their name, the parish directory or electronic database can be searched. That will tell if the person is or is not a parishioner.

If the caller is not a parishioner, ask how he or she chose this parish for their sacramental needs. Generally the next step for sacramental preparation—especially baptisms and weddings—involves a meeting with the pastor, deacon, or a member of the parish staff. During this meeting, the pastor or pastoral associate can encourage their registration in the parish as a means of bringing these people into the life and activities of the church. They can be encouraged to register, attend Mass, and participate in the parish for more than just the occasional sacrament.

4.9. Parish Voice Mail

If a parish is using an automated telephone system, make sure it is user-friendly. Remember that people unfamiliar with the parish will have to navigate the system. A directory of just names or positions will not suffice. A good rule to follow is to list staff members by name, position, and extension: "Youth Minister, Joy Anderson, extension 267."

Reciting the extension number before the name ("Press 267 to be connected to Joy Anderson, the Director of Youth Ministry") is too confusing. With that system callers have to note each extension number until they finally hear the correct name and then remember the extension number that preceded the name. If each staff member has an individual voice mailbox, have each person record his or her name and extension for the mailbox. This will save the caller from having to listen to the entire menu each time they call the parish office; they will know the person's extension number from their last call.

Automatic voice mail systems can also be programmed to provide mailboxes for specific ministries, schedule times, directions, office hours—even one with the events for that week. When setting up these mailboxes and listing them in the directory, remember that it is better to say, "To hear the Mass schedule, press 5" rather than "Press 5 to hear the Mass schedule."

Whether a parish uses a receptionist or voice mail is not the issue. The issue is whether or not the system is user-friendly—and whether or not it communicates effectively the mission and message, procedures and programs of the parish.

The same is true of parish bulletins, directories, newsletters, announcements, e-mail messages, and Web sites. Make sure that they all communicate the message of warmth, service, and spirituality that is the hallmark of the parish.

Public Information:
The Key to Publicizing Your Parish

A parish census form and database will contain a wealth of information about registered parishioners. But many other people live within the parish boundaries, work in the neighborhood, attend area schools, or are served by care centers, hospitals, and nursing homes. Part of the "marketing mix" used to promote any parish should include programs, activities, or services that encourage more participation by local residents and are intended both to serve the people's needs and attract new members.

There are several ways to reach out to non-members in the larger community. There are also ways to obtain public information and other valuable data about the people who live and work near the parish church.

5.1. Public Records

Local governments (city, township, county) have volumes of data available to the general public. Most of this information comes from the property tax roles or the recorder of deeds. Most governments print an annual listing of property owners, property addresses, and tax assessments. Some municipalities also release home sales data on a regularly scheduled basis, such as monthly or quarterly.

All of this data is public information, so using it violates no privacy laws. If the local government does not typically release the collective data, contact the office and ask how to obtain a copy of the information, preferably on a computer disk.

You can then merge all of the new addresses with the parish census database. Delete from the new list the addresses that match those of current parishioners. This provides the address of every non-member in the neighborhood. Turn this information over to the parish marketing committee or evangelization team.

5.2. Census Data

Every ten years the U. S. Census Bureau collects a wealth of statistics about all the people across the country. This government agency divides and subdivides the information into neighborhoods, ZIP code zones, and similar small geographic areas. While this data does not provide names and addresses, it does provide information about the people who live near the parish church. It focuses on age, race, family size, type of housing unit, household income, level of education, and many other different statistics.

Of course, this is more than just interesting information. This is a valuable link to the potential individuals and families who can be served by the parish and share their gifts and talents with the local parish community and the wider church.

Several firms have developed geodemographic models to analyze the census data. Many are familiar with the saying "Birds of a feather flock together," but other diverse species can also live in close proximity. These geodemographic models can help you understand who lives in your neighborhood. What is the average income? How old are the residents? Do most of them have children? Census data can also be linked to product choices and lifestyle variables. One such company, Claritas, provides a free analysis of your local ZIP code (see Appendix B for contact information). Many other sources are also available on the Internet. It just takes a little surfing.

5.3. Local Institutions

Not every parishioner is part of a two-parent, two-child, two-car family living in a single-family home with an attached garage and a well-manicured lawn. Even beyond couples or singles living in condominiums or apartments, parishioners—or potential parishioners—may live in college dormitories, senior residences, nursing homes, boarding houses, single-room occupancy buildings, and residential hotels. Not every such building is huge. It may look like a private home or apartment building, but contain many people.

Finding these buildings may take some detective work using the phone book and other local listings. Once they are located, however, it is time to send notices, bulletins, and newsletters inviting the occupants to participate in the events, services, and activities of the parish. It is also appropriate to survey the residents of these buildings to determine their special needs and see if they can be served by the parish staff or its corps of volunteers.

Remember that in many such institutions, the employees may be more interested and able to attend parish services than the residents. When they are scheduled to work on a weekend or holy day they will appreciate knowing that there is a church nearby that they can attend before or after work, especially if they have a long commute.

5.4. Area Visitors

Is there a hospital, nursing home, or similar building or facility in the area? If someone came to an institution like this to visit a friend or relative, would they be able to know the name of the local parish church, the Mass schedule, and the directions to the church? The same information should be available to a guest at a local hotel.

Enter the addresses, and ideally a contact person, for each such institution or establishment into the parish database. Code these sites in such a way that they receive information about events and activities that is pertinent to their clients.

5.5. Neighborhood Agencies

The parish is not an island unto itself and does not operate in a vacuum. There are sure to be other churches in the community. There may be other Catholic parishes, other Christian communities, and possibly non-Christian congregations. In every community there are is a wealth of social service agencies.

When a parish maintains a database of such organizations and exchanges information about programs and services with other groups, the people of the parish are better served. As others learn about the social, service, and spiritual activities of the local Catholic parish, attendance and the general level of participation often increase.

If the parish has the space, it can be beneficial to offer civic, community, and service groups and agencies a meeting place. Many an Alcoholics Anonymous member's first contact with a parish church came from attending an AA meeting in a school basement or church hall.

A parish can welcome many organizations to its facilities, including blood drives, osteoporosis screenings, Girl Scouts, Boy Scouts, and many others. They serve not only people in the local community but also serve the parishioners. Opening the social hall to these organizations also opens the church doors to them.

Inviting the neighborhood crime watch group to meet with the local police officers in a parish meeting room might lead to increased surveillance of the parish property, and might also bring someone back to the church who has not attended in many years but who was welcomed to a neighborhood meeting in the parish hall.

5.6. Civic Events

A parish calendar can be filled with multiple activities for every day of the year to serve each segment of its total population. That is good, but it is better when some of the activities on the parish calendar reach beyond the parish boundaries to include participation in civic and community events.

The parish might consider entering a team in the local sports league, having a float in the neighborhood parade, or sponsoring a booth at a neighborhood festival. Putting together a church processional banner or float is a fun way to bring together parishioners of all ages.

Have the evangelization or welcoming committee in full force ready to answer questions at the local farmer's market, Fourth of July celebration, or town picnic. Consider preparing an information table or booth. Collect names and addresses, but most importantly, be a welcoming presence. Some might even walk among the crowd distributing a leaflet or flier.

On such days consider opening the church for a guided tour. This is an opportunity to teach guests about the faith as the symbolism in the artwork, windows, sacramental furnishings, and sacred space is explained.

5.7. Ecumenical Collaboration

Ecumenical activities can expand the level of religious understanding among parishioners and enrich the faith life of the entire parish. Thanksgiving services, clothing drives, Reformation Sunday, Church Unity Octave, food pantries, and homeless shelters are often conducted on a community or interchurch basis. Make the extra effort to host these events occasionally.

If the parish database lists the church affiliation of the non-Catholic partner in a marriage, ecumenical activities can provide a special opportunity for couples and families to work together. Reach out to these couples and let them be the ones to forge the ecumenical relationships between churches based on the relationship they already have as husband and wife.

5.8. Local Publicity

Effective utilization of local newspapers is another important ingredient in getting the parish and its activities known in the community. There are two ways to use the newspaper: through a paid advertisement and through free publicity. The advantage of the paid advertisement is that the parish has complete control over the look and content of the message it wants to deliver. The disadvantage is that the parish must pay for the advertisement. Free publicity is the mirror opposite: it's free but the parish loses control.

Check the local newspaper and take note of what other churches and synagogues are doing. If the parish is holding similar events or programs, send a news release to the paper. Reading about what other religious groups are doing can also provide the parish planning committee with additional ideas for the congregation.

To improve the likelihood that an editor will notice a press release, take time to meet with the editor or a staff reporter. Learn and follow the paper's guidelines. Find out what type of information or stories they find interesting. Find out the schedule they follow for publishing notices and the advance notice they need to prepare the story.

5.9. Real Estate Agents

As homes are bought and sold within the parish, new potential members arrive. The new residents are young and old, single and married, with or without children. Something has attracted them to the neighborhood, whether it is other family members or friends who already live in the area, or a new job or relocation. Often some of the first contact they make in the area is with a local real estate agency.

Make sure local real estate agents know

about the church and school and their major programs and initiatives. As home sales increase in the spring and summer, consider offering an "open house" for local real estate agencies. Send invitations to all the area agents, not just one invitation to each office. Develop a presentation asking key staff members to speak about their programs.

If the school plays a major role in the parish consider holding the session there. Be sure to highlight what sets the school apart from the others in the area. Aside from the obvious spiritual component of a church-sponsored school, maybe you have a great music program or art studio.

Provide each agent with a flier or packet of information about the parish and its school and other essential programs and services. Make the real estate agent a partner in evangelization! Offer the same flier or packet to the chamber of commerce, neighborhood business group, or community center. Make sure that someone on the staff stops by periodically to replenish the supply of brochures.

5.10. New Members

Each of the ideas in this chapter offers another way to reach out to potential new members. Whether they be new residents of the area, short-term residents like students, or people seeking to find or rediscover their relationship with God, they may be open to Jesus' directive to spread the Good News—if only someone welcomes them.

Local merchants use the data and the contacts mentioned above to expand their business and get out the message about their service or product. The parish church can send a similar welcome letter. Keep in mind that not all of the property owners or residents of an area will be Catholic. The letter should reinforce the positive contribution that the church makes to the local community.

Beyond sending a welcome letter to new residents of the area, consider sending the parish newsletter to the entire geographic community at least once a year. Send a special Christmas or Easter invitation in the form of a card listing the times of the services.

Use block captains or confirmation candidates to canvass the neighborhood and deliver newsletters door to door. Purchase or prepare a brochure like the one from the Catholic Conference of Illinois that is available from Liturgy Training Publications (LTP). *Discover the Catholic Church* presents a concise description of the Church and answers many of non-Catholics' misunderstandings about our faith and practice.

Conclusion

While some people will ring the rectory doorbell to register, ask for collection envelopes, and volunteer to serve in various capacities, such a person is the exception rather than the rule. The more ways a parish reaches out to its neighbors, the more chances there are that a new member will be found. The suggestions in this chapter are just the beginning. Be creative and spread the word.

Sacraments and Funerals:
The Key to Changing Your Parish

There are a hundred uses for a parish database. There are far fewer events that change a parish database. Someone moves into the area or joins the parish. Someone else moves away. A child is born or adopted. A parishioner receives a sacrament or enters eternal life. Besides necessitating a change in the database, such events should also bring about a change in the person and the parish community.

The recommendations in this chapter are not tied directly to the parish database, yet planning for each event can be made smoother using the database. The key, of course, is not the almighty database, but the actual events that can have a positive impact on the life of the parish and its members.

6.1. Introduce Baptismal Candidates

Most parishes direct special care to the baptism of infants. The new mom and dad, and sometimes the godparents, are asked to attend a baptismal preparation class led by a deacon, parish educator, or volunteer couple. While fewer and fewer parishes celebrate the baptism during a weekend liturgy, they often take place immediately after the last Mass on Sunday mornings. If that is the case, invite the family and their guests to attend Mass and introduce the baby. Parishioners see the expectant mother at church but might miss out on news of the birth. By announcing the celebration of the baptism and introducing the couple and the baby, parishioners can offer their congratulations.

On the feast of the Baptism of the Lord—and this is where the parish database comes in handy—celebrate a baptism reunion for the families of all the infants who were baptized in the past year. Call them forward and offer a special blessing.

6.2. Celebrate Engagements

During the course of marriage preparation, the engaged couple will be advised to attend Mass—especially if they have not been present at the parish weekend liturgies. They may have been away at college or just moved into the parish and not really feel welcome or involved. Rather than just listing their names in the traditional banns of marriage, introduce the engaged couples to the congregation at a weekend liturgy.

Present them to the congregation and ask everyone to pray for them as they prepare for their wedding day. What a strong affirmation the couple will feel knowing that an entire congregation is praying for them.

6.3. Prepare for Weddings

As part of the preparation for their marriage, the office staff and the pastoral team need to work together and develop a seamless system to handle all of the inquiries, questions, forms, rehearsals, etc. What preparation options are available to the couple? How many forms must they complete? Is there a different stipend for parishioners and non-parishioners? At what point do they meet with the music director?

To help couples complete the preparation, consider preparing a printed booklet of rules, regulations, procedures, and contact information. It answers all the questions mentioned above and many other "who, what, where, when, why, and how" questions that always arise.

Consider using the parish database to find couples married from five to ten years who would serve as "marriage mentors" or "sponsor couples" to work with the couples before and after their wedding. These mentor/sponsor couples attend training sessions and then commit to work with one or two engaged couples over the course of a year.

The parish database also comes in handy when planning a reunion for all couples married within the past year. Remember to invite the mentor/sponsor couples and work with them to provide input and discussion along the lines of a "what's working, what's not working" seminar at the reunion event.

6.4. Welcome Death

At funerals we pray for eternal rest for those who have lived a good life and now enjoy their eternal reward. Those of us who are alive and healthy hesitate to talk about our own mortality. Parishes can assist their parishioners by offering end-of-life directive seminars, pre-need funeral planning meetings, and will clinics and estate seminars.

Announce the events to all parishioners through numerous channels. Use the database to invite personally anyone over a certain age or on the list of parishioners who are homebound or in nursing homes. For the latter two groups, suggest that they send a family member on their behalf if they are unable to attend.

Consider conducting a three-week program once or twice a year depending on the demographics of the parish.

- *Week 1:* Gather a team that includes the pastor and medical and legal professionals. Explain "do not resuscitate" orders, power of attorney for health care, living wills, and the various procedures that are possible to prolong life. Explain the Church's position on respirators, feeding tubes, and other extraordinary means.
- *Week 2:* Have a local attorney or a representative from the (arch)diocesan development office present a clinic on wills and durable power of attorney for property. It is also appropriate to mention how someone can leave a portion of their estate to the local church or a favorite charity.
- *Week 3:* Have the pastor, pastoral associate, or music director explain how to select readings, prayers, and music for the funeral liturgy.

6.5. Plan for Funerals

The parish office is often the first place a person calls after notifying family members of a death. As such, the staff needs to have resources at hand to assist the family in the wake and funeral planning process. Grief needs immediate attention. It is not enough for the bereavement team to be available only during the evening.

The parish office should have one of the many practical resources for planning a funeral that is both complete and yet simple. Not every staff person can handle such a delicate matter, but having these materials available is a good start for the family until someone can meet with them. The key, of course, is to help people at their own level. Some families are totally unfamiliar and unprepared to offer their thoughts about readings and readers, songs, and personal remembrances. It may be due to the circumstances of the death or to their level of participation in the church. Other families—or the deceased person himself or herself—will indicate clear preferences for readings, songs, and symbols of remembrance.

Spiritual Activities:
The Key to Enriching Your Parish

Once a parish has a complete and current database, it can determine who might be in need of particular spiritual assistance. Who is homebound? Who is beyond the normal age but has not yet received a particular sacrament?

With little cost and lots of organization, a parish can offer many priceless spiritual services to targeted segments of its parishioners. Here are a number of spiritual and devotional activities for which the parish database can be used to reach the intended parishioners.

7.1. Audio Tapes for Shut-ins

Ministers of care bring the eucharistic Body of Christ to the homebound. They can also bring the local body of Christ with them as they bring news of the parish community in a copy of the parish bulletin. But there is more that can be done. Ministers of care can bring a recorded tape of the Sunday homily and the music that was played and sung at Mass. Many church audio systems can be adapted to include a cassette tape recorder. If time permits the minister and the homebound person can listen to the tape together, or the tape can be left and listened to during the week. It is a terrific way to connect homebound parishioners to the worshiping community and serve as a prayerful reminder of the community that is praying for them.

The parish database should contain a list of homebound parishioners. Those not receiving regular visits from a minister of care can have a tape mailed to them occasionally.

> Taped homilies and music from special occasions can also be made available to parishioners who have moved away but still hold the parish community in their heart. Locate them through the parish database.

7.2. Printed Copies of Homilies

Tape recording a homily is not always possible or practical. When that is the case, ask the homilist to provide a printed copy of the homily. While many priests and deacons may not prepare a fully written text of their homily, they might share an annotated outline or summary.

In a parish where there are several Masses and different preachers, it may be sufficient and most practical to have just one preacher share his thoughts on a particular weekend.

> The distribution process for printed homilies can be the same as for audiotapes, although possibly made available to a larger list of recipients. Either way, the parish database speeds the process and ensures that the proper people receive this spiritual support.

7.3. The Book of Intentions

Each Sunday the Church prays the general intercessions. We pray for the world, the Church, religious and civil leaders, local needs, those who are sick or have died, and for "those intentions held silently in our hearts and minds." Prayer walls or a book of intentions provide another avenue for the community to express its needs.

A book of intentions placed at a shrine in the church offers a quiet, reflective place for those in need of prayers to put into words their cares and concerns. The book of intentions can be brought forward during the general intercessions or as part of the procession along with the gifts.

The person who prepares the general intercessions can peruse the book of intentions and compose intentions based on the general needs expressed in the book. A parish could decide to burn the book of intentions in the Easter fire, reminding those in attendance that "my prayers rise like incense" (Psalm 141:2).

> Use many of the means of communication mentioned in this book—parish bulletin, newsletter, e-mail update—to remind people periodically about the book of intentions. Remind people on an annual basis at least of the purpose and placement of the book. For special occasions like All Souls Day or at a time of crisis or in wartime, invite people to list people involved with the particular situation.

7.4. Daytime "Table Talk" Programs

A parish staff can be a storehouse of religious and spiritual information. Consider scheduling a weekday or monthly morning "table talk" with parishioners and a staff member or ministry chairperson who can provide a valuable venue for discussion and feedback. These monthly chats can have a focus, such as explaining changes to current parish programs or soliciting community input for new spiritual, social, or service programs. The sessions can be spiritual, religious, or practical.

These meetings will put staff members in direct contact with a group of parishioners in a way that is more valuable than the hurried, quick words and "mini-meetings" that occur standing in the vestibule of church or in the parking lot. Make sure the coffee is brewed and the sweet rolls are fresh!

> The parish database points out who might be available at a particular time of the day, based on their job schedule. It also allows the target audience for such an event to be segmented: women over fifty, anyone over seventy, mothers with children under the age of six.

7.5. Pray for One Another

A parish community prays together on weekends at the liturgy when it gathers in the church building. There may be ways to encourage people to pray at others times of the day and week.

One parish conducted a "Month of Prayer." Every household was mailed the name of another household and asked to pray for them each day during that month. A printed prayer was included with the invitation, along with suggestions of three times when it might be convenient to recite the prayer—in the morning, as part of the family's grace before the main meal, or at bedtime.

Use the parish database to match families based on criteria determined by the parish staff. You could have singles pray for other singles, older people pray for families with young children, people from one part of the parish pray for people in another area, or new parishioners pray for those who have lived an entire lifetime in the parish.

Care needs to be taken to guarantee people's privacy, so you may not want to list anything more than the name of the parishioner. You may also want to make this a voluntary program. Have people fill out a card with their name and an intention or spiritual need. Then exchange the cards among the people who filled one out.

Praying for others can be a special ministry of the elderly and homebound. Many senior members of a parish have been active in parish associations and organizations their entire life and want to remain so but can no longer attend Mass or other services. Consider a "Ministry of Praise" in which at-home "ministers" pray for the needs of the parish. Have a parish staff member or minister of care prepare a newsletter that contains the needs of the parish to be prayed for during that month.

7.6. Unified Parish Meeting Prayer

Parish groups can sink into a routine when they plow into their agendas, forgetting that they gather firstly as a Christian community and secondly as the finance committee or school board. All parish meetings should begin with prayer asking the Spirit's guidance for the work at hand, the people gathered for the meeting, and the people of the parish who will be affected by the activity of this group.

As a sign of unity and solidarity among the many boards, committees, and groups within a parish, a meeting prayer can be developed that all groups will use during that week. It can relate directly or indirectly to the Sunday worship. This prayer might include intentions for the parish community. It might contain a scripture passage selected for its relevance to current events or the Gospel for the coming Sunday. Whatever is chosen, it should be a unified prayer for all groups for the entire week.

Depending on the resources available in a parish for composing a weekly prayer, a simple start would be to read and reflect on the Gospel for the coming weekend. If the number of people in attendance permits, allow some time for personal reflection on the Gospel and end with intercessory prayer.

Use the parish database and calendar to know which groups are meeting and to which meeting facilitators and conveners the prayer needs to be distributed.

7.7. Annual Parish Faith Celebrations

The annual parish feast day or similar parish anniversary celebrations are a great way to gather people for a spiritual event. Whether the celebration is a special Mass or a series of faith celebrations (and social gatherings that could include a parish carnival, catered dinner, or "block party"), be creative in the execution. Events as important as these take many hours of preparation, so consider allowing the celebration to be more than just one event.

School children can do research and make presentations on the patron saint. Older members can share verbal and written remembrances of the parish. Even if it is not a "major" anniversary, an annual celebration can be an occasion of grace. One parish celebrates its patron saint each year with a children's play about their patron and a simple catered buffet dinner for the whole parish. One must be mindful if the patron saint was chosen when the parish was one ethnic group and has since changed to another ethnic group. The Nativity of our Lord Parish may decide that it does not need another Christmas event, but might celebrate on the feast of the Annunciation because it heralded the conception of Christ that bore fruit at the Nativity.

For major golden anniversary and centennial celebrations, local newspapers, the dedication book, and subsequent anniversary books are a gold mine of information about parish history. Major celebrations can be designed to last for an entire year or even extend for more than a year. One parish had a three-year centennial celebration. The laying of the cornerstone was commemorated one year, the dedication of the church the following year, and the third year was the actual beginning of the parish centennial.

> More than just the current parishioners should participate in an annual celebration. Use the parish database and sacramental records to invite former parishioners, alumni, graduates of the school, and couples who were married at the parish.

7.8. Catholic Family Time

Today's society exerts a lot of tension on families. With "soccer moms and dads" arranging car pools to everything from band practices to study groups, families are pulled in many directions. They often do not have the time or the ability to gather as a family to reflect on a particular feast or season.

Consumerism also directs families away from holy days and sacred seasons. Christmas advertising begins the day after Halloween, completely bypassing Advent and ending on Christmas Day, just as the church begins its celebration of Christmas. Retail stores begin their Easter push on Ash Wednesday. Just as Christians are trying to become more aware of a time of conversion, merchandisers are trying to convert us to consume more candy, more clothes, and even family cruises over the Sacred Triduum.

The parish can be the place that Christians can reclaim their traditions. Breakfast with Santa may not be appropriate during Advent. Likewise, an Easter egg hunt on Holy Saturday might be rushing the season.

Consider developing a Catholic family time spiritual program. It can be a quarterly event to bring the whole family together to work on projects that are appropriate to the church's calendar and not to the retailer's business goals.

The Advent family time might include creating an Advent wreath or celebrating one of the Advent feast days like St. Nicholas, Our Lady of Guadalupe, or St. Lucy. Plan a children's activity that can be completed during the holiday recess from school to continue the celebration of Christmas.

Other family projects at the parish could include a Christmas caroling party on the Feast of Stephen (December 26) or a display of parishioners' crèches on the Feast of the Epiphany, when everyone brings the Three Kings from their nativity set.

Similar seasonal events can be scheduled for Lent/Easter and also for the Ordinary Times of the year.

> When these programs are planned and promoted, keep in mind that they should not be limited just to the people who come to Mass or read the bulletin. Use the parish database to target those who do not attend church regularly. Provide them with a religious message to balance the many commercial messages they receive from secular society. Send one information packet to families with children and another with different activities for single adults and older and childless couples.

7.9. Church Tour

Many churches are veritable museums. They don't even have to be old, although older churches tend to be more ornate. As part of your parish's feast day celebration, develop a guided tour explaining the signs and symbols, statues and windows in your church. Both young and old enjoy these tours. A self-guided tour booklet can be created that can be placed in the parish pamphlet racks for visitors and longtime parishioners to use at their leisure.

A parish historian is an invaluable source of information, and so are dedication and anniversary books. The (arch)diocesan archives are another source of history and information, as are local newspapers. Parishioners also might have mementos, wedding pictures, and newspaper clippings that can become an important part of a parish "museum" collection.

As activities in parishes and schools tend to decline in the summer months, excerpts from the tour book can be excellent bulletin filler. This is more than a chance for parishioners to learn about their surroundings; the biblical and biographical information about the events depicted in statues and stained glass and the symbols used in the altar, baptismal font/pool, and ambry for the holy oils are an opportunity for catechesis as well. If your city or town has a founder's day celebration or other such community event, remember that your parish is also part of that history and open your doors, too.

> The parish database will help you find the oldest parishioners as well as those who received the initiation sacraments decades ago. They have lived the parish history for many decades and might be an interesting source of information.

7.10. Anointing Service

As people grow older their needs and expectations in life change. For those who can attend Mass, offer a communal anointing. Ministers of care can arrange rides for those who are able to come to this special Mass. Arrange the seating so that those to be anointed are seated at the end of the aisle. Have medical personnel present in case someone becomes ill during the service.

> Use the parish database to invite people over a certain age and anyone known to be homebound or receiving visits from a minister of care.

7.11. All Souls Memorial

Consider gathering on or near the feast of All Souls at the beginning of November for an evening of remembrance for the families and friends of those who were buried from your church in the previous year. Prepare special music and readings for the service. All are invited to place a picture of their departed loved ones on the altar of remembrance, often near the statue of Saint Joseph, the patron of a happy death. Leave the pictures in place for the entire month of November.

Be sure to remind people to put their name, address, and telephone number on the back of the photo and the name of the deceased on the front. Have the ministers of care, who so frequently brought Communion to the deceased in their final illness, prepare a reception for the entire congregation to be enjoyed after the service. While the service may last just about an hour, it will remain in their hearts for them to cherish for years.

> Use the database to locate the listing of all those who have died in the past year. The parish database can also indicate the nearest living relative of each deceased parishioner to whom the invitation can be sent.

Conclusion

No matter the spiritual activity undertaken by the parish, it is likely that the parish database can be a great asset. Whether it lists the people eligible for the program, or even before that helps to determine the need for a particular event, or enables parish staff to reach a select audience, the parish database is vital to all spiritual programs.

Service Activities:
The Key to Humanizing Your Parish

A parish may be primarily a source of spiritual nourishment and growth, but it also has a dimension of service. Jesus reminded the apostles to clothe the naked, feed the hungry, and give drink to the thirsty. Now expressed as works of mercy, these actions also include visiting the sick, comforting the dying, and similar actions performed in Jesus' name.

The suggestions provided here can help a parish to enliven its service activities and find ways to use the parish database to reach the necessary people.

8.1. Ministry Fair

A parish ministry fair can create a fun, carnival-like experience to bring three major groups together: program coordinators, program volunteers, and potential program users. Think of it as a parish trade show where the services of the parish are showcased.

Set a date far in advance on the parish calendar that will not conflict with any other parish event and schedule no other events on that day. The seasonality of parish programs will assist in determining the best date—when people are likely to volunteer at a time suitable for the start of many activities.

At the ministry fair, each service activity group should have its own table with handouts, posters, sign-up sheets, and volunteers to staff the table. Hang a sign for each table on the wall above the table or from the ceiling so that it can be seen across the room rather than taping the sign to the front of the table where it will be blocked by the crowds eager to learn about your ministry. If food is served (always a good lure), consider having something at each table instead of at a central location. This will encourage people to visit all the tables.

Use the database to generate a postcard to everyone on your parish mailing list. Alternately, gather enough volunteers to call everyone in the parish. Twenty phone calls per volunteer is certainly a manageable number. Provide the caller with a script to ensure that the correct message is given—and be optimistic about the results.

8.2. Parish "Telecare"

As parishes grow and people's lives become busier, consider staying in touch by calling each parishioner once a year. Have a brief list of questions to assess their needs and interests. To accomplish this task, prepare a well-worded script with specific questions that will yield multiple-choice or short-answer responses. Work ahead of time with the callers to prepared responses for anticipated negative comments.

Information from the parish database should be available to the callers so that they can be knowledgeable about the family situation. It should not be a "cold call" but should be a friendly conversation with a fellow parishioner.

Even in a parish with good communication and active ministries, a parish telecare call will yield information about a parishioner who has been sick for a long time or a family that has been struck by a tragedy. All the programs imaginable are of little value if the parishioners do not know they exist or perhaps are too sick to make the parish aware of their needs.

Depending on the size of the parish, expect that this project will take anywhere from a week to several months to complete. The team for this project should include not only staff members and the pastor, but also ministry coordinators and other volunteers who are well aware of what programs are currently available.

8.3. Neighborhood Networks

A network can be developed to assist fellow parishioners in specific geographic areas of the parish. Working like a political organization, the parish can be divided up into smaller segments. Each area captain—even down to a neighborhood block level—can help keep the connection between parishioners and the parish in place. When an older parishioner is not seen at his or her usual weekend Mass and when the regular contribution envelope is missing, the neighborhood network volunteer can make a phone call or ring a doorbell just to chat and make sure things are okay.

> The parish database should be able to provide printouts of parishioners in a specific geographic area like a certain street or streets with addresses in a certain numerical range.

8.4. Total Care Network

While staying in touch with neighbors who are church members can have positive benefits for the church, the neighborhood, and the people, offering specialized care for individual needs is another valuable service parishioners can offer to each other.

If a couple suffers a miscarriage, stillbirth, or neonatal death, they may find great consolation from talking with another couple who has experienced the same tragedy. A widow who lost her husband to Alzheimer's disease might have a wealth of practical information to share with a fellow parishioner whose spouse has just been diagnosed with the dread illness. Even though catechumens have a sponsor as they proceed through the RCIA process, they might benefit from speaking with a neophyte from several years ago.

Stepparenting is another area where those who have been successful at this difficult task can offer words of encouragement to those who are just setting out on this life adventure.

The possibilities are endless. A special field in the parish database could contain information about specific life situations that a person has experienced and that he or she would be willing to speak about with another parishioner facing the same challenge.

The actions that can take place are amazing and overwhelming. In one instance an expectant mom in the choir was put on bed rest for three months. Between her neighborhood network, fellow choir members, and other women who had experienced difficult pregnancies, meals were provided to her, her husband, and their three-year-old son for the entire duration of her pregnancy and then for some time after her daughter was born.

8.5. Freezer Meals

There was a time when people brought food to the home of a family in which a person had died. This custom was a way of showing that people cared and also served a practical need. As people grieved, planned the funeral, and welcomed out-of-town mourners, they needed food.

In a modern-day version of this practice,

consider stocking a "freezer bank" with meals cooked by volunteers. Once a month or quarter, depending on the parish size and the number of volunteers, people could be asked to cook a meal that can be frozen and stored in the "freezer bank" for later use. Whenever there is a death or family crisis, the meals could be used. Meals not used at the parish within a freezer-safe time could be given to a local soup kitchen or homeless shelter.

8.6. Transportation Network

The parish telecare calls may show that some people, most often the elderly but occasionally the poor, do not have a convenient, affordable way to get to essential doctor and hospital visits or to church, stores, and the bank. A chauffeur ministry can be developed.

Volunteer drivers shuttle people to Mass, parish events, doctor appointments, the grocery store, or on other errands. Check with the insurance carrier or risk management provider about liability insurance for the volunteer driver and the church.

8.7. Senior Service

Retirees tend to be younger, more mobile, and more highly trained that ever before. Parish helpers can be recruited from among the parish senior citizens. Retired seniors with professional skills could be organized to assist parishioners, especially fellow seniors, who are unable to afford the help they need. Other seniors are eager to serve as volunteer grandparents for families with young children when the actual grandparents live far away.

The parish school or religious education program might have a use for seniors as tutors. The parish office is often a great place for seniors to assist in preparing mailings, answering the phone, or recording information for the parish database.

Yet another group of senior volunteers might be those "do-it-yourselfers" who volunteer their time doing odd jobs and minor home repairs for elderly and disabled parishioners, or at the parish buildings and grounds.

8.8. Volunteer Gardeners

The maintenance staff can be expected to take care of the parish grounds as well as the buildings. On the other hand, people can volunteer to take care of different sections of the parish property. One parish has an outdoor shrine to Mary that was donated by a family as a memorial to their son who died in World War II. More recently, a shrine to St. Francis of Assisi was added to the church garden.

For a number of years the local Brownie and Girl Scout troops have planted flowers around these shrines as a service project each spring. Once planted, the care then belongs to someone else. As a social activity, consider beginning a gardener's club in which members have no meetings or dues to pay but commit to maintaining an area of the parish grounds.

> To encourage more participants, use census data to form two new groups, "Mary's Gardeners" and "Francis' Caretakers." Invite the Marys of the parish to care for her garden and ask men named Francis, Frank, or Franz to care for the other. This new service project will allow these men and women to lend a hand to a project that has a personal appeal.

8.9. Signs of the Times

At a time of personal or familial crisis, many people turn to the church before they think of talking with a counselor. While the parish staff may not have the training to offer the necessary guidance, a parish can be a referral center.

The church vestibule is often the place to post information about the parish (the current and previous week's bulletin, parish newsletter) and education and ministerial programs. This can also be the place to publicize programs offered at a neighboring parish or through the diocesan office as well as local community events.

Keep in mind that the most effective pro-life posters are not the ones that remind people that abortion is murder, but the ones that offer pregnancy testing and adoption counseling.

One thoughtful parish did not limit its posters to the vestibule for all to see. It placed a poster in the women's restroom offering a crisis line phone number for battered women.

If your space permits, multiple bulletin boards can be hung to allow a board for each age segment of your congregation. For example, the teen board could include information about activities designed around their interests, promotional material for Catholic colleges and vocational opportunities, and information about the local teen crisis center.

8.10. Babysitting Service

If the analysis of the parish database shows that there is a large population of infants and toddlers, a nursery might be appropriate for use during Mass or other parish events. The nursery may be staffed by paid or volunteer babysitters. This is also a good service project for confirmation candidates.

As a secondary service, if a well-trained group of babysitters is developed through some type of course of instruction or certification, their names can also be given to parents looking for childcare at their home during either parish or non-parish events. Of course, check with the diocesan risk management office or parish insurance carrier to make sure there are no liability issues with either having a babysitting service during Mass or offering names of parish young people as potential babysitters.

8.11. Estate Seminar

Death is part of living, but often elderly parents do not talk with their adult children about their final wishes or things that need to be addressed in an emergency. Consider inviting people to an estate planning seminar. Contact the (arch)diocesan office of planned giving for recommendations of people with legal and financial backgrounds who can conduct such a program. The focus is on making sure that peo-

ple understand the legal implications of not having a will and thus the benefits of preparing a last will and testament. Other topics explained at such a seminar include durable power of attorney and health care power of attorney. Estate taxes are also covered. At the end of the seminar the presenter gently reminds the audience that they might also want to consider leaving a gift to the parish that they have supported throughout their lives.

This can also be the time to speak to people about making their funeral directives known. Several religious publishers have inexpensive booklets that help people consider issues concerning medical treatment, finances, death, and funerals. Send one to everyone over the age of sixty-five. Ask a local funeral home to pay for the books and the mailing costs. In consideration for the expense, invite the firm to place a self-adhesive business card on the inside front cover.

> Use the parish database to target people over a certain age and send them special invitations to the will and estate seminar and any other programs or sessions about aging, the spirituality of illness, death, or funeral planning.

8.12. All Are Welcome

A popular hymn proclaims, "All are welcome in this place." No matter which service ministries or what volunteer programs are organized, the key is to welcome all people to the parish and to the services it offers. A church needs a welcoming persona. As a church creates and refines ministries, develops service programs, and reaches out to its complex and varied group of parishioners, the simplest of smiles and friendly voices will be the binding agent to make it all come together. If the staff is welcoming and that message is conveyed to volunteers in parish ministries, the people in the pews and up and down the streets of the parish will embody that same spirit.

Social Activities:
The Key to Enlivening Your Parish

'**C**hurch" does not happen only on Sunday, nor is it anticipated just on Saturday evenings. The building of a community, one of the key components of a parish or church, happens every day of the week, every week of the year. Here are a few suggestions about some social activities that have succeeded in one form or another at many parishes.

Announcing these events or recruiting people to participate can be made easier in each instance by mining the parish database for potential participants.

9.1. Musical Review

Books have been written about why Catholics can't sing. That doesn't stop parishes from staging musicals and variety shows. Choir members sing religious texts each Sunday, and probably can also belt out a good Broadway tune. Performing in a parish musical can give choir members—and those singing parishioners who don't belong to the choir—another opportunity to share their gifts with the parish and maybe earn the applause that isn't often heard at Mass. A parish musical can also draw on the talents of other parishioners for set design and construction, costume making, and publicity for the event. Conducting a parish musical can bring togeth-er a wide range of volunteers, involving everyone from budding child actors to seasoned ticket takers.

9.2. People's Parish History and Cookbook

Parishes and women's clubs everywhere have published cookbooks. Consider publishing a history of the parishioners along with the cookbook. As the women's club or home and school association members solicit recipes for the parish cookbook, they can also collect stories of parish life.

A recipe has a special personal touch if it is introduced with a story; for example: *My mother made this casserole for every church potluck. Once she brought something else, no one can remember what, but everyone missed her regular dish. In fact, it wasn't regular at all—it was her "signature" dish that everyone loved.*

Parish stories can be mixed and blended in with the recipes. Creating parish cookbooks is an easy task since there are numerous companies whose business is to help organizations publish cookbooks. They offer direction on how to collect the recipes and additional useful information in preparing the cookbook.

These cookbooks become cherished heirlooms with each printing. With each generation come new recipes to add to the treasured favorites.

9.3. Christmas Caroling and Party

Hosting a Christmas party during Advent is business as usual for most parishes, but it also takes away from the spirit of the season. Consider inviting parishioners to come together a few days after Christmas. If enough people come, break into several caroling groups.

> Use the parish database to develop lists of homes where parishioners are homebound. Send a group of carolers to pay them a visit to share holiday cheer in song.
>
> After the singing, invite everyone back to the parish for refreshments. Plan on some time for more songs together.

9.4. Volunteer Recognition Celebration

Volunteers are the backbone of parishes. Without their dedicated service, parishes could not exist. Consider hosting a volunteer appreciation dinner. Volunteers do not expect anything but a "thank you." All the more reason to host such an event. It will be necessary to cater the event, have it off-campus, or use the paid parish staff as the hosts so that volunteers are not asked to volunteer to assist with their own recognition dinner.

Entire books have been written on the care of volunteers. Beyond hosting a party, there are many other ways to recognize the invaluable service provided by dedicated volunteers. Consider writing a personalized thank-you note to volunteers at Thanksgiving. It's not a time people would normally expect a thank-you note but it is an appropriate time. Another recognition possibility involves creating a Volunteer of the Year award to be pre-

sented as part of an annual parish celebration for volunteers.

If the parish budget does not allow for a dinner, consider inviting volunteers to receive their "Just Desserts." The paid parish staff can serve desserts donated or purchased from local bakeries. Consider providing childcare as a way to enable as many parents as possible to attend without the expense of babysitters.

> The parish database will have the information for alerting and inviting all the parish volunteers to the celebration in their honor.

9.5. Newcomer Events

To help ease new parishioners into parish life, plan activities that reach out to the newcomers. These events offer a great way for the new members to begin meeting other families.

Host a new members' brunch, dinner, or appetizer party. Depending on how many new members register, this event might need to be held monthly or quarterly. Holding it just once a year is too infrequent. Since new members often spend some time evaluating and attending the parish before actually completing a parish registration form, they will not consider themselves to be "new" parishioners if the new-member event takes place many months or a year after they began attending the church.

If the newcomer event is a Sunday brunch, include a special blessing for the new members at the Mass. It will be invigorating for longtime parishioners to see the new life being added to the community.

The event becomes more meaningful if someone writes the family names of all newcomers on a welcome banner or on a decorated cake. It is also a good idea to ask staff members or volunteers to "adopt" one of the new families and invite the new parishioners to all appropriate parish events in the coming year.

9.6. Adopt a Family

It is imperative to take the extra effort to remind new members why they joined the parish. Send personal invitations to parish events during their first year as registered parishioners. Long-term parishioners know that "everybody" comes to the parish block party or that the annual dinner dance and auction is the highlight of the parish social year, but newcomers won't. Reaching out to invite them and give them a little history will go a long way toward helping them weave themselves into the fabric of parish life.

Matching a new parishioner with a veteran member of similar age and background can be a good way for the new parishioner to feel welcome. The host may invite the new individual or family to parish events, and possibly even to dinner at their home where they can meet other parishioners.

9.7. Gather Students' Parents

Hosting a special educational evening for parents of the students in the parish school or religious education program can require tremendous work and planning. Such events often do not attract many parents. Instead, plan a coffee social during religious education classes. Instead of dropping the students off at school and returning in an hour or so, invite the parents to gather in the parish hall for a little socializing. A brief presentation could also be made that parallels what their children are learning.

For a parochial school, plan a coffee during the first period of school. As parents bring their children to school, they can pick up a cup of coffee and spend some time socializing with other parents before returning home or heading off to the office. Ask the school principal to host the gathering and be available to the parents. This event could also be an opportunity to inform parents about upcoming school events.

9.8. Business Associates Group

Depending on the demographics of the parish, it might be appropriate to start a business group. Such a group can have several benefits for a parish and its members.

Invite entrepreneurs and professionals to list their business or practice through the business associates group. Parishioners may feel more comfortable using a business run by a parishioner rather than one they select at random from the telephone book.

If enough parishioners work in a central business district, a parish could organize a lunch meeting on a monthly basis. The presentations and discussions could include business matters or reflective faith sharing. In the Archdiocese of Chicago, the First Friday Club of Chicago draws hundreds of business and religious leaders to its monthly lunchtime speaker series.

Business associates could also be brought together to foster networking and develop business relationships among parishioners' companies. The business associates can also offer career counseling or a job referral network for those in transition or between careers.

9.9. Something for Everyone

While a parish cannot be all things to all people, it can have programs and social activities that meet many of the diverse needs of its parishioners. Social activities are more than just good times. It was a wise old pastor who remarked, "I'm not sure of the connection, but I know that the longer the lights stay on at the parish gym on weekday nights, the more people I see at church on Sunday morning."

Appendix A:
Confidential Parish Census Form

To order copies of this form for your parish, call the J. S. Paluch Help Desk at 1-800-621-6732 and ask for the Paluch Church Management System Confidential Census Form, JSP 540010.

CONFIDENTIAL CENSUS FORM

Dear Parishioner:

Thank you for taking the time to complete and return this parish census form as early as possible. This information enables us to serve you better, and run our church more efficiently in the Catholic community.

Start by listing, on the next page, all the members in your family, and then continue to answer the questions to the best of your knowledge. You'll find special instructions provided where needed; however, if you need additional help, please call our parish office and we will be glad to assist you.

This information will be held in the strictest confidence for pastoral use
------- ONLY -------

General Family Information

Family Name _____ Salutation _____

Address _____ Apartment #_____

City _____ State _____ Zip _____

Home Phone _____ Unlisted Phone _____ E-mail _____

| **OFFICE USE ONLY:** | Carrier Route # _____ | Parish Area _____ | Registry Date _____ | Envelope # _____ |

Family Member Information

	Last Name	First Name	M.I.	Nickname	Family Relationship
1.					
2.					
3.					
4.					
5.					
6.					

Detailed Family Member Information

Instructions: Please fill in the appropriate circles for your assigned family member # (from section above).

	Family Member #1	Family Member #2	Family Member #3	Family Member #4	Family Member #5	Family Member #6
Work Telephone:	( )___ ____	( )___ ____	( )___ ____	( )___ ____	( )___ ____	( )___ ____
Mailing List:	○ Yes ○ No	○ Yes ○ No	○ Yes ○ No	○ Yes ○ No	○ Yes ○ No	○ Yes ○ No
Nationality: Fill in the circles that best describe your ethnic background.	○ African Amer. ○ British ○ Chinese ○ Filipino ○ French ○ German ○ Greek ○ Hispanic ○ Irish ○ Italian ○ Korean ○ Polish ○ Vietnamese Other _____	○ African Amer. ○ British ○ Chinese ○ Filipino ○ French ○ German ○ Greek ○ Hispanic ○ Irish ○ Italian ○ Korean ○ Polish ○ Vietnamese Other _____	○ African Amer. ○ British ○ Chinese ○ Filipino ○ French ○ German ○ Greek ○ Hispanic ○ Irish ○ Italian ○ Korean ○ Polish ○ Vietnamese Other _____	○ African Amer. ○ British ○ Chinese ○ Filipino ○ French ○ German ○ Greek ○ Hispanic ○ Irish ○ Italian ○ Korean ○ Polish ○ Vietnamese Other _____	○ African Amer. ○ British ○ Chinese ○ Filipino ○ French ○ German ○ Greek ○ Hispanic ○ Irish ○ Italian ○ Korean ○ Polish ○ Vietnamese Other _____	○ African Amer. ○ British ○ Chinese ○ Filipino ○ French ○ German ○ Greek ○ Hispanic ○ Irish ○ Italian ○ Korean ○ Polish ○ Vietnamese Other _____
Language: If you speak a second language besides English, please fill in the appropriate circle.	○ Chinese ○ French ○ Greek ○ Italian ○ Korean ○ Polish ○ Spanish ○ Swedish ○ Tagalog ○ Vietnamese Other _____	○ Chinese ○ French ○ Greek ○ Italian ○ Korean ○ Polish ○ Spanish ○ Swedish ○ Tagalog ○ Vietnamese Other _____	○ Chinese ○ French ○ Greek ○ Italian ○ Korean ○ Polish ○ Spanish ○ Swedish ○ Tagalog ○ Vietnamese Other _____	○ Chinese ○ French ○ Greek ○ Italian ○ Korean ○ Polish ○ Spanish ○ Swedish ○ Tagalog ○ Vietnamese Other _____	○ Chinese ○ French ○ Greek ○ Italian ○ Korean ○ Polish ○ Spanish ○ Swedish ○ Tagalog ○ Vietnamese Other _____	○ Chinese ○ French ○ Greek ○ Italian ○ Korean ○ Polish ○ Spanish ○ Swedish ○ Tagalog ○ Vietnamese Other _____

	Family Member #1	Family Member #2	Family Member #3	Family Member #4	Family Member #5	Family Member #6
Date of Birth: M-Month D-Day Y-Year	MM/DD/YYYY	MM/DD/YYYY	MM/DD/YYYY	MM/DD/YYYY	MM/DD/YYYY	MM/DD/YYYY
Baptized? **Baptized at:** (Church Name)	○ Yes ○ No _____	○ Yes ○ No _____	○ Yes ○ No _____	○ Yes ○ No _____	○ Yes ○ No _____	○ Yes ○ No _____
Date of Baptism:	MM/DD/YYYY	MM/DD/YYYY	MM/DD/YYYY	MM/DD/YYYY	MM/DD/YYYY	MM/DD/YYYY
Received 1st Communion?	○ Yes ○ No	○ Yes ○ No	○ Yes ○ No	○ Yes ○ No	○ Yes ○ No	○ Yes ○ No
Date of 1st Communion:	MM/DD/YYYY	MM/DD/YYYY	MM/DD/YYYY	MM/DD/YYYY	MM/DD/YYYY	MM/DD/YYYY
Confirmed?	○ Yes ○ No	○ Yes ○ No	○ Yes ○ No	○ Yes ○ No	○ No	○ Yes ○ No
Date Confirmed:	MM/DD/YYYY	MM/DD/YYYY	MM/DD/YYYY	MM/DD/YYYY	MM/DD/YYYY	MM/DD/YYYY
Marital Status:	○ Married ○ Remarried ○ Separated ○ Divorced ○ Single ○ Widow ○ Widower Other _____	○ Married ○ Remarried ○ Separated ○ Divorced ○ Single ○ Widow ○ Widower Other _____	○ Married ○ Remarried ○ Separated ○ Divorced ○ Single ○ W Other _____	○ Married ○ Remarried ○ Separated ○ Divorced ○ Single ○ Widow ○ Widower Other _____	○ Married ○ Remarried ○ Separated ○ Divorced ○ Single ○ Widow ○ Widower Other _____	○ Married ○ Remarried ○ Separated ○ Divorced ○ Single ○ Widow ○ Widower Other _____
Date of Marriage:	MM/DD/YYYY	MM/DD/YYYY	MM/DD/YYYY	MM/DD/YYYY	MM/DD/YYYY	MM/DD/YYYY
Married by a Priest/Deacon? **Maiden Name:**	○ Yes ○ No _____	○ No _____	○ Yes ○ No _____	○ Yes ○ No _____	○ Yes ○ No _____	○ Yes ○ No _____
Denomination:	○ Catholic ○ Baptist ○ Episcopalian ○ Jewish ○ Lutheran ○ Methodist ○ Presbyterian Other _____	○ Catholic ○ Baptist ○ Episcopalian ○ Jewish ○ Lutheran ○ Methodist ○ Presbyterian Other _____	○ Catholic ○ Baptist ○ Episcopalian ○ Jewish ○ Lutheran ○ Methodist ○ Presbyterian Other _____	○ Catholic ○ Baptist ○ Episcopalian ○ Jewish ○ Lutheran ○ Methodist ○ Presbyterian Other _____	○ Catholic ○ Baptist ○ Episcopalian ○ Jewish ○ Lutheran ○ Methodist ○ Presbyterian Other _____	○ Catholic ○ Baptist ○ Episcopalian ○ Jewish ○ Lutheran ○ Methodist ○ Presbyterian Other _____
Converted?	○ Yes ○ No	○ Yes ○ No	○ Yes ○ No	○ Yes ○ No	○ Yes ○ No	○ Yes ○ No
Homebound?	○ Yes ○ No	○ Yes ○ No	○ Yes ○ No	○ Yes ○ No	○ Yes ○ No	○ Yes ○ No
Receiving Communion?	○ Yes ○ No	○ Yes ○ No	○ Yes ○ No	○ Yes ○ No	○ Yes ○ No	○ Yes ○ No
Request Home Visit?	○ Yes ○ No	○ Yes ○ No	○ Yes ○ No	○ Yes ○ No	○ Yes ○ No	○ Yes ○ No

SAMPLE

	Family Member #1	Family Member #2	Family Member #3	Family Member #4	Family Member #5	Family Member #6
School attending or school last attended:	_____	_____	_____	_____	_____	_____
Education Level: Please fill in the highest grade level you have achieved.	○ Pre-school 3 ○ Pre-school 4 ○ Kindergarten —*Grade School*— ○ 1st ○ 2nd ○ 3rd ○ 4th ○ 5th ○ 6th ○ 7th ○ 8th —*High School*— ○ Freshman ○ Sophomore ○ Junior ○ Senior —*College Year*— ○ 1st ○ 2nd ○ 3rd ○ 4th Other _____	○ Pre-school 3 ○ Pre-school 4 ○ Kindergarten —*Grade School*— ○ 1st ○ 2nd ○ 3rd ○ 4th ○ 5th ○ 6th ○ 7th ○ 8th —*High School*— ○ Freshman ○ Sophomore ○ Junior ○ Senior —*College Year*— ○ 1st ○ 2nd ○ 3rd ○ 4th Other _____	○ Pre-school 3 ○ Pre-school 4 ○ Kindergarten —*Grade School*— ○ 1st ○ 2nd ○ 3rd ○ 4th ○ 5th ○ 6th ○ 7th ○ 8th —*High School*— ○ Freshman ○ Sophomore ○ Junior ○ Senior —*College Year*— ○ 1st ○ 2nd ○ 3rd ○ 4th Other _____	○ Pre-school 3 ○ Pre-school 4 ○ Kindergarten —*Grade School*— ○ 1st ○ 2nd ○ 3rd ○ 4th ○ 5th ○ 6th ○ 7th ○ 8th —*High School*— ○ Freshman ○ Sophomore ○ Junior ○ Senior —*College Year*— ○ 1st ○ 2nd ○ 3rd ○ 4th Other _____	○ Pre-school 3 ○ Pre-school 4 ○ Kindergarten —*Grade School*— ○ 1st ○ 2nd ○ 3rd ○ 4th ○ 5th ○ 6th ○ 7th ○ 8th —*High School*— ○ Freshman ○ Sophomore ○ Junior ○ Senior —*College Year*— ○ 1st ○ 2nd ○ 'th Other _____	○ Pre-school 3 ○ Pre-school 4 ○ Kindergarten —*Grade School*— ○ 1st ○ 2nd ○ 3rd ○ 4th ○ 5th ○ 6th ○ 7th ○ 8th —*High School*— ○ Freshman ○ Sophomore ○ Junior ○ Senior —*College Year*— ○ 1st ○ 2nd ○ 3rd ○ 4th Other _____
Church Attendance: Please fill in the circle that best describes your church frequency.	○ Daily ○ Weekly ○ Monthly ○ Occasionally ○ Seldom ○ Holidays ○ Other	○ Daily ○ Weekly ○ Monthly ○ Occasionally ○ Seldom ○ Holidays ○ Other	○ Daily ○ Weekly ○ Monthly ○ Occasionally ○ Seldom ○ Holidays ○ Other	○ Daily ○ Weekly ○ Monthly ○ Occasionally ○ Seldom ○ Holidays ○ Other	○ Daily ○ Weekly ○ Monthly ○ Occasionally ○ Seldom ○ Holidays ○ Other	○ Daily ○ Weekly ○ Monthly ○ Occasionally ○ Seldom ○ Holidays ○ Other
Employed?	○ Yes ○ No	○ Yes ○ No	○ Yes ○ No	○ Yes ○ No	○ Yes ○ No	○ Yes ○ No
Occupation:	_____	_____	_____	_____	_____	_____
Employer's Name:	_____	_____	_____	_____	_____	_____
Address:	_____ _____	_____ _____	_____ _____	_____ _____	_____ _____	_____ _____
Groups: Please use the enclosed sheet to select the Groups code numbers.	___, ___, ___, ___, ___, ___, ___, ___, ___	___, ___, ___, ___, ___, ___, ___, ___, ___	___, ___, ___, ___, ___, ___, ___, ___, ___	___, ___, ___, ___, ___, ___, ___, ___, ___	___, ___, ___, ___, ___, ___, ___, ___, ___	___, ___, ___, ___, ___, ___, ___, ___, ___
Skills: Please use the enclosed sheet to select the Skills code numbers.	___, ___, ___, ___, ___, ___, ___, ___, ___	___, ___, ___, ___, ___, ___, ___, ___, ___	___, ___, ___, ___, ___, ___, ___, ___, ___	___, ___, ___, ___, ___, ___, ___, ___, ___	___, ___, ___, ___, ___, ___, ___, ___, ___	___, ___, ___, ___, ___, ___, ___, ___, ___

Additional comments:

J.S. Paluch Co, Inc ©
540010

Thank you again for your participation and continued support for our parish.

Appendix B:
Resources

This list of associations and publications contains many practical, accessible resources. Business managers and parish staff members can refer to them for additional background or for assistance in implementing the suggestions and ideas presented throughout this book.

Associations and Organizations

National Association of Church Personnel
    Administrators
100 East Eighth Street
Cincinnati, OH 45202
513-421-3134
E-mail: nacpa@nacpa.org
Web site: www.nacpa.org

National Association for Lay Ministry
6896 Laurel St. NW
Washington, DC 20012
202-291-4100
E-mail: nalm@nalm.org
Web site: www.nalm.org

National Catholic Development Conference
86 Front Street
Hempstead, NY 11550-3667
516-481-6000 or toll-free 888-879-6232
E-mail: glehmuth@ncdcusa.org
Web site: ncdcusa.org

National Catholic Stewardship Council
1275 K Street NW, #980
Washington, DC 20005-4006
202-289-1093
E-mail: ncstewar@aol.com

National Council for Catholic Evangelization
415 Michigan Avenue NE, Suite 90
Washington, DC 20017
800-786-6223
E-mail: director@catholicevangelization.org
Web site: www.catholicevangelization.org

National Pastoral Life Center
18 Bleecker Street
New York, NY 10012-2404
212-431-7825
E-mail: nplc@nplc.org
Web site: www.nplc.org

United States Conference of Catholic Bishops
3211 Fourth Street NE
Washington, DC 20017-1194
202-541-3000
Web site: www.usccb.org

Business and Marketing for Parishes

Archdiocese of Chicago. *Parish Communications Handbook.* Chicago: Office of Communications, P.O. Box 1979, Chicago, IL 60690.

Kotler, Philip, Rath, Gustave, Shawchuck, Norman, and Wren, Bruce. *Marketing for Congregations: Choosing to Serve People More Effectively.* Nashville, TN: Abingdon Press, 1992.

Nelson, Bob. *1001 Ways to Reward Employees.* New York: Workman Publishing, 1994.

Steinfels, Margaret, Untener, Kenneth, and Wall, John. *Are Catholics Active Enough in Their Church?* Proceedings of a Foundations and Donors Interested in Catholic Activities symposium. Washington, DC: FADICA, 1992.

Zech, Charles E. Why *Catholics Don't Give . . . and What Can Be Done About It.* Huntington, IN: Our Sunday Visitor, 2000.

Demographics

Claritas U.S. Offices
Corporate Headquarters
5375 Mira Sorrento Place, Suite 400
San Diego, CA 92121
800-866-6520
Web site: www.claritas.com

Evangelization

Brennan, Patrick J. *Parishes That Excel: Models of Excellence in Education, Ministry, and Evangelization.* New York: Crossroad, 1992.

———. *Re-Imagining Evangelization: Toward the Reign of God and the Communal Parish.* New York: Crossroad, 1996.

Hater, Robert J. *Catholic Evangelization: The Heart of Ministry.* Denville, NJ: Dimension Books, 2001.

Pable, Martin W. *Reclaim the Fire: A Parish Guide to Evangelization.* Notre Dame, IN: Ave Maria Press, 2002.

Periodicals

Church is a quarterly publication of the National Pastoral Life Center (see Associations above). www.nplc.org/magazine

Leadership: A Practical Journal for Church Leaders is published quarterly by Christianity Today International, 465 Gunderson Drive, Carol Stream, IL 60188 (800-777-3136). www.LeadershipJournal.net

Ministry & Liturgy is published 10 times a year by Resource Publications, 160 E. Virginia Street, Suite 290, San Jose, CA 95112 (408-286-8505). www.rpinet.com/ml/

Pastoral Life: The Magazine for Today's Ministry is published 11 times a year by the Society of Saint Paul, Box 595, Canfield, OH 44406-0595. www.albahouse.org/plcenter

Today's Parish is published 10 times a year by Twenty-Third Publications, Box 180, Mystic, CT 06355-0180 (800-321-0411). www.twentythirdpublications.com

U. S. Catholic is published monthly by Claretian Publications, 205 W. Monroe, Chicago, IL 60606 (800-328-6515). www.uscatholic.org

Your Church: Helping You with the Business of Ministry is published bi-monthly by Christianity Today International, 465 Gunderson Drive, Carol Stream, IL 60188 (800-777-3136). www.christianitytoday.com/cbg/

Stewardship

Champlin, Joseph M. *Grateful Caretakers of God's Many Gifts: A Parish Manual to Foster the Sharing of Time, Talent, and Treasure (Sacrificial Giving Program).* Collegeville, MN: Liturgical Press, 2002.

Clements, C. Justin. *Stewardship: A Parish Handbook.* Liguori, MO: Liguori Publications, 2000.

Kielbasa, Marilyn. *Stewardship: Creating the Future.* Winona, MN: Saint Mary's Press, 2003.

McNamara, Patrick H. *Called to Be Stewards: Bringing New Life to Catholic Parishes.* Collegeville, MN: Liturgical Press, 2003.

Smith, Colleen. *Catholic Stewardship: Sharing God's Gifts.* Huntington, IN: Our Sunday Visitor, 2001.

United States Catholic Conference of Bishops. *Stewardship: A Disciple's Response.* Washington, DC: United States Catholic Conference, 1993.

Web Sites

www.Quotationspage.com
A good source when you need a quote and don't have a book of quotations handy.

www.nccbuscc.org/nab/bible/
This is the Bible search from the United States Conference of Catholic Bishops. A good source to find the perfect quote to include in any parish-wide mailing.

Workshop Presenters

Center for Ministry Development
P.O. Box 699
Naugatuck, CT 06770
Web site: www.cmdnet.org

The Parish Evaluation Project
Rev. Thomas Sweetser, SJ (Director)
3195 South Superior Street
Milwaukee, WI 53207
Phone: 414-483-7370
Fax: 414-483-7380
E-mail: pep@pitnet.net
Web site: www.pepparish.org